A Paines Plough and Liv

Broken Biscuits

by Tom Wells

The first performance of *Broken Biscuits* took place on
5 October 2016 at Live Theatre, Newcastle upon Tyne

 Paines Plough theatre   ARTS COUNCIL ENGLAND Community Foundation

Broken Biscuits

by Tom Wells
with songs by Matthew Robins

Cast

MEGAN	Faye Christall
HOLLY	Grace Hogg-Robinson
BEN	Andrew Reed

Production Team

Direction	James Grieve
Songs	Matthew Robins
Design	Lily Arnold
Lighting Design	Joshua Pharo
Sound Design	Dominic Kennedy
Costume Supervisor	Lou Duffy
Producer (Paines Plough)	Hanna Streeter
Producer (Live Theatre)	Graeme Thompson
Production Manager	Drummond Orr
Assistant Director	Anna Ryder
Company Stage Manager	Aimee Woods
Technical Stage Manager	Ben Pavey
Stage Management Placement	James Rosen
Movement Coach	Polly Bennett
Voice Coach	Elspeth Morrison
Set Builder	Harrogate Theatre

Tour Dates

2016

05–22 October	Live Theatre, Newcastle
25–29 October	The Drum, Theatre Royal Plymouth
01–05 November	Hull Truck Theatre
08–12 November	Stephen Joseph Theatre, Scarborough
15–19 November	Crucible Studio, Sheffield Theatres
25–26 November	Tobacco Factory Theatre, Bristol
29 November–03 December	Birmingham Repertory Theatre

TOM WELLS (Writer)

Tom is from Kilnsea, East Yorkshire. Plays include: *Folk* (Birmingham Rep/Hull Truck Theatre/Watford Palace Theatre); *Jumpers for Goalposts* (Paines Plough/Watford Palace Theatre /UK tour, 2013/14); *Cosmic* (Ros Terry/Root Theatre, East Yorkshire tour, 2013); *The Kitchen Sink* (Bush Theatre, 2011, winner of the Most Promising Playwright – Critics' Circle, 2011 and the 2012 George Devine Award); *Me, As A Penguin* (West Yorkshire Playhouse, 2009 and Arcola Theatre/UK tour, 2010) and *About a Goth* (Paines Plough/Òran Mór, 2009).

Ben & Lump, which Tom wrote as part of the *Coming Up* season (Touchpaper) was broadcast on Channel 4 in 2012 and his play *Jonesy* was broadcast on Radio 4. He has also written three pantos for the Lyric Hammersmith.

Tom is currently under commission to the Drum Plymouth, the Royal Court and the National Theatre.

MATTHEW ROBINS (Songs)

Matthew Robins is an artist and musician from the West Country. Combining live animation, shadow puppetry, short films, music, and made-up games he regularly tours with his band, performing stories about animals, death, monsters, the ocean, and love.

As a film-maker Matthew has recently worked on commissions from the Barbican, Opera North, Led Bib, Dumbworld (*Peter, Lily and the Nose,* winner of the audience choice award at the Capital Irish Film Festival), and made animations for Tori Amos (*The Light Princess* at the National Theatre) and Phil Collins (*Tomorrow is Always Too Long,* for the 2014 Glasgow Commonwealth Games).

Matthew's recent work for theatre includes writing and performing *Flyboy is alone again this Christmas,* and *Lullaby –* both for the Barbican, and designing and making puppets for *Something Very Far Away* for the Unicorn Theatre, *A Most Peculiar Wintry Thing* for the Ark in Dublin, and *Laila –* a new musical at Watford Palace Theatre.

A collection of Matthew's animations and installations is on permanent display at the Science Museum in London in the new *Information Age* gallery.

Matthew is currently adapting Ted Hughes' *The Iron Man* for the Unicorn Theatre, and he is a regular musical guest on the BBC radio show *CLICK.*

'Robins' music is in the indie-folk vein. Peppered with pop inflections, the tunes slip easily between tempos that vary from klezmer-like jauntiness to a lilting waltz. The tales they convey are odd slivers of surreal whimsy.' *The Times*

'The whole thing feels like a silent movie in which every aspect has been created by a wayward child genius' *Guardian*

FAYE CHRISTALL (Megan)

Faye is making her debut with Paines Plough and trained at the American Academy of Dramatic Arts in New York.

Theatre credits include: *Gone Viral* (St James); *One Flew Over the Cuckoo's Nest* (Edinburgh Fringe).

Film credits include: *Cute Little Buggers 3D* and *Awake.* Workshops include: *The Band* (Tricycle). Faye is also part of the Cirque du Soleil Company.

GRACE HOGG-ROBINSON (Holly)

TV includes: The regular role of Beth Kennedy in *The Coroner: Series 1 & 2* (BBC1 & BBC Worldwide) as well as appearances in *Casualty* (BBC1); *Camping* (Sky Atlantic); *Diary of a Snob* (Nickelodeon); *Doctors* (BBC1) and *Suspects* (Channel 5).

Film includes: *Edge of Tomorrow* (Warner Bros.); *Birdhouse* (NFTS); *Candy Floss* (HAUS Pictures) and *The Nest* (Beyond Fiction). This marks Grace's stage debut.

ANDREW REED (Ben)

Andrew was born in South Tyneside. He trained with The Customs House, South Shields and the Theatre Royal Newcastle. Credits include: *The Fifteen Streets, Drama, Baby, Takeaway* (The Customs House, South Shields); *Scrapbook* (Live Theatre, Newcastle); *The Machines, 13* (Theatre Royal Newcastle and on tour).

JAMES GRIEVE (Direction)

James is Joint Artistic Director of Paines Plough. He was formerly co-founder and Artistic Director of nabokov, and Associate Director of the Bush Theatre.

For Paines Plough James has directed *The Angry Brigade* by James Graham, *Jumpers for Goalposts* by Tom Wells, *Hopelessly Devoted* and *Wasted* by Kate Tempest, *An Intervention* and *Love, Love, Love* by Mike Bartlett, *Fly Me To The Moon* by Marie Jones, *Tiny Volcanoes* by Laurence Wilson, *You Cannot Go Forward From Where You Are Right Now* by David Watson, *The Sound of Heavy Rain* by Penelope Skinner, *Organised* by Lucinda Burnett and *Happiness* by Nick Payne for BBC Radio 3.

Further credits include a new production of *Les Misérables* for Wermland Opera in Karlstad, Sweden; *Translations* (Sheffield Theatres/ETT/Rose – winner Best Production, UK Theatre Awards 2014); *66 Books: A Nobody* by Laura Dockrill, *The Whisky Taster* by James Graham, *St Petersburg* by Declan Feenan and *Psychogeography* by Lucy Kirkwood (Bush); *Artefacts* by Mike Bartlett (nabokov/Bush, national tour & Off-Broadway); *Kitchen, Bedtime for Bastards* and *Nikolina* by Van Badham (nabokov).

LILY ARNOLD (Design)

Training: Wimbledon College of Art.

Theatre and opera: *The Jew of Malta*; *King Lear*; *The Taming of the Shrew*; *The Rape of Lucrece* (RSC); *The Solid Life of Sugar Water, Yellowface* (NT temporary space); *The Sugar-Coated Bullets of the Bourgeoisie, Peddling* (Arcola/HighTide Festival*); So Here We Are* (HighTide Festival/Royal Exchange*); The Fruit Trilogy* (West Yorkshire Playhouse/Rambert Studio*); Jeramee, Hartleby and Ooglemoore* (Unicorn); *Forget Me Not* (Bush); *Putting the Band Together Again* (Summer Streets and Edinburgh Festivals); *Things Will Never be The Same Again* (Tricycle); *The Box of Photographs, Minotaur* (Polka); *Up and Out Christmas Sprout* (Northern Stage); *Tomcat* (Southwark Playhouse); *Blake Remixed* (West Yorkshire Playhouse); *Beached* (Marlowe Studios/Soho); *The Edge of our Bodies, Gruesome Playground Injuries* (Gate); *World Enough and Time* (Park); *The Boss of It All* (Assembly Roxy/ Soho);

A Season in the Congo, The Scottsboro Boys (Young Vic, Clare Space); *Happy New* (Trafalgar Studios); *Opera Scenes* (National Opera Studio); *Red Handed* (The Place, London). www.lilyarnold.com

JOSHUA PHARO (Lighting)

Joshua works as a Lighting and Projection Designer across theatre, dance, opera, music, film & art installation.

Recent credits include: *Burning Doors* (Belarus Free Theatre); *Carmen* UK tour (OperaUpClose); *The Future* (Company Three); *Contractions* (Sheffield Crucible); *Julie* (Northern Stage); *We're Stuck!* (China Plate); *Giving* (Hampstead); *Iphigenia Quartet, In The Night Time (Before The Sun Rises), Medea* (Gate); *The Rolling Stone* (Orange Tree); *Glass Menagerie* (Nuffield, as Video Designer); *The Merchant of Venice, Wuthering Heights, Consensual* (Ambassadors); *The Crocodile* (Manchester International Festival); *One Arm* (Southwark Playhouse); *The Trial Parallel, A Streetcar Named Desire Parallel* (Young Vic); *Amadis De Gaulle* (Bloomsbury); Beckett season (Old Red Lion); *The Deluge* (UK tour, Lila Dance); *Usagi Yojimbo* (Southwark Playhouse); *Pioneer* (UK tour, Curious Directive); *I'd Rather Goya Robbed Me Of My Sleep, No Place Like Home* (The Gate); *Thumbelina* (UK tour, Dancing Brick). www.joshuapharo.com

DOMINIC KENNEDY (Sound)

Dominic is a Sound Designer and Music Producer for performance and live events, he has a keen interest in developing new work and implementing sound and music at an early stage in a creative process. Dominic is a graduate from Royal Central School of Speech and Drama where he developed specialist skills in collaborative and devised theatre making, music composition and installation practices. His work often fuses found sound, field recordings, music composition and synthesis. Dominic has recently designed for and collaborated with Paines Plough, Goat and Monkey, Jamie Wood, Gameshow, Manchester Royal Exchange, Engineer, Outbox, Jemima James and Mars Tarrab. Recent installation work includes interactive sound design for Gingerline (pop-up restaurant pioneers) and the launch of Terry Pratchett's *The Shepherd's Crown*. Recent theatre credits include: *With a Little Bit of Luck* (nationwide tour); *The Human Ear* (Roundabout); *The Devil Speaks True* (The Vaults/nationwide tour); *Run* (New Diorama); *ONO* (Soho); *Our Teacher is a Troll* (Roundabout); *Crocodiles* (Manchester Royal Exchange); *Karagular* (Shoreditch Town Hall).

ANNA RYDER (Assistant Director)

Anna is a freelance director and is a Live Lab Associate Artist at Live Theatre.

Directing credits: *Get Yourself Together* by Josh Coates (Royal Exchange/tour); *A Living* by Caroline Liversidge (ARC Stockton/tour); *Rendezvous, What She Would Have Wanted* by Ian Mclaughlin, *Trolley Boy* by David Raynor, *Not For Shale* by Jo Kirtley (Live Theatre).

Assistant/Associate Director credits: *Get Carter* adapted by Torben Betts (Northern Stage: winner of JMK regional bursary), *Miracle: An Opera For Sunderland* by David Almond (Music in The Minster); *Man On The Moon* adapted by Zoe Cooper (New Writing North); *Wet House* by Paddy Campbell (Live Theatre); *ENRON* (Northern Stage); *The GB Project* by Kate Craddock and Steve Gilroy (Live Theatre and Northern Stage at St Stephens); *Tallest Tales from the Furthest Forest* by Susan Mulholland (Northern Stage).

The national theatre of new plays

Paines Plough is the UK's national theatre of new plays. We commission and produce the best playwrights and tour their plays far and wide. Whether you're in Liverpool or Lyme Regis, Scarborough or Southampton, a Paines Plough show is coming to a theatre near you soon.

'The lifeblood of the UK's theatre ecosystem' *Guardian*

Paines Plough was formed in 1974 over a pint of Paines bitter in The Plough pub. Since then we've produced more than 130 new productions by world renowned playwrights like Stephen Jeffreys, Abi Morgan, Sarah Kane, Mark Ravenhill, Dennis Kelly and Mike Bartlett. We've toured those plays to hundreds of places from Manchester to Moscow to Maidenhead.

'That noble company Paines Plough, de facto national theatre of new writing' *Telegraph*

Our Programme 2015 saw 12 productions by the nation's finest writers touring to 84 places from Cornwall to the Orkney Islands; in village halls and Off-Broadway, at music festivals and student unions, online and on radio, and in our own pop-up theatre Roundabout.

With Programme 2016 we continue to tour the length and breadth of the UK from clubs and pubs to lakeside escapes and housing estates. Roundabout hosts our most ambitious Edinburgh Festival Fringe programme ever and brings mini-festivals to each stop on its autumn tour. We're extending our digital reach by live streaming shows and launching our free Come To Where I'm From app featuring over 100 audio plays.

'I think some theatre just saved my life' @kate_clement on Twitter

Paines Plough are

Joint Artistic Directors	James Grieve
	George Perrin
Senior Producer	Hanna Streeter
General Manager	Aysha Powell
Producer	Francesca Moody
Assistant Producer	Sofia Stephanou
Administrator	Simone Ibbett- Brown
Marketing and Audience Development Officer	Jack Heaton
Production Assistant	Harriet Bolwell
Finance and Admin Assistant	Charlotte Walton
Technical Director	Colin Everitt
Trainee Director	Anna Himali Howard
Big Room Playwright Fellowship	Sam Steiner
Production Assistant Placement	Sonia Martins
Admin Placements	Amelia Lock & Charlotte Young
Press Representative	The Corner Shop
Designer	Thread Design
	Michael Windsor-Ungureanu

Paines Plough Limited is a company limited by guarantee and a registered charity.
Registered Company no: 1165130
Registered Charity no: 267523

Paines Plough, 4th Floor, 43 Aldwych, London WC2B 4DN
+ 44 (0) 20 7240 4533
office@painesplough.com
www.painesplough.com

 Follow @PainesPlough on Twitter

 Like Paines Plough at facebook.com/PainesPloughHQ

 Follow @painesplough on Instagram

Donate to Paines Plough at justgiving.com/PainesPlough

 Supported by
ARTS COUNCIL ENGLAND

Live Theatre is recognised as one of the great new-writing theatres on the international stage. Based in Newcastle upon Tyne it is deeply rooted in its local community and produces work as varied and diverse as the audiences it engages with.

As well as championing the art of writing for stage by producing and presenting new plays, Live Theatre uses theatre to unlock the potential of young people and finds, nurtures and trains creative talent.

The theatre is a beautifully restored and refurbished complex of five Grade II listed buildings with state-of-the-art facilities in a unique historical setting including both cabaret style theatre and studio theatres. In 2016 Live Garden, an outdoor performance space, and Live Tales, a creative writing centre for children and young people, were added.

Founded in 1973, Live Theatre is a national leader in developing new strategies for increasing income and assets for the charity. To sustain and extend its artistic programme it has diversified its income streams to include Live Works, the purchase and development of commercial property for rental income; an award-winning gastro pub The Broad Chare; The Schoolhouse a hub for creative businesses, and on-line interactive playwriting course www.beaplaywright.com.

Live Theatre is grateful for the support of Arts Council England and the Newcastle Culture Investment Fund through the Community Foundation, and its many other friends and supporters.

For more information visit **www.live.org.uk**

Live Theatre is operated by North East Theatre Trust Limited, a registered Charity No. 513771

 Follow @LiveTheatre on Twitter

 Like Live Theatre at facebook.com/livetheatre

 Follow @LiveTheatreNewcastle on Instagram

Live Theatre are

Chief Executive	Jim Beirne
Artistic Director	Max Roberts
Operations Director	Wendy Barnfather
Administrator to the Directors	Clare Gowens

Finance, Events & Venue Hire

Finance Manager	Antony Robertson
Finance Officer	Catherine Moody

Marketing

Marketing Manager	Cait Read
Marketing Manager	Claire Cockroft
Marketing and Press Officer	Lisa Campbell
Marketing and Press Officer	Melanie Rashbrooke
Box Office Administrator	John Ramsay

Development

Director of Enterprise & Development	Lucy Bird
Development Manager	Lizzy Skingley

Education & Participation

Director of Education & Engagement	Helen Moore
Associate Director	Paul James
Resident Drama Worker	Toni McElhatton
Resident Drama Worker	Christina Castling

Literary

Literary Manager	Gez Casey
Creative Producer	Graeme Thompson
Administrator	Degna Stone

Production & Technical

Production Manager	Drummond Orr
Technical Manager	Dave Flynn
Technician	Craig Spence

House Management

House Management	Carole Wears
Deputy House Manager	Michael Davies
Duty House Manager	Ben Young
Duty House Manager	Lewis Jobson
Duty Manager	Sarah Matthews

Friends of Live Theatre play a key role in helping us to nurture new writing and to deliver world-class plays. Our **Best Friends** are:

Anthony Atkinson, Noreen Bates, Jim Beirne, Michael and Pat Brown, Dorothy Braithwaite and Paul Callaghan, George Caulkin, Michael and Susan Chaplin, Sue and Simon Clugston, Helen Coyne, Chris Foy, Robson Green, Lee Hall, John Jordan, John Josephs, Annette Marlowe, Madelaine Newton, Elaine Orrick, Ian and Christine Shepherdson, Margaret and John Shipley, Shelagh Stephenson, Sting, Alan Tailford, Graeme and Aly Thompson, Paul and Julie Tomlinson, Nick and Melanie Tulip, Alison Walton, Kevin Whately, Lucy Winskell. And those who choose to remain anonymous.

For more information about the Friends scheme call **(0191) 269 3499** or visit **www.live.org.uk/friends**
Live Theatre is grateful for the support of Arts Council England and Newcastle City Council as well as its many other supporters and Friends.

BROKEN BISCUITS

Tom Wells

For James Grieve,
who fell in the canal

'Mis-shapes, mistakes, misfits
Raised on a diet of broken biscuits.'

Pulp

Characters

MEGAN, *sixteen*
BEN, *sixteen*
HOLLY, *sixteen*

This text went to press before the end of rehearsals and so may differ slightly from the play as performed.

1.

MEGAN*'s shed.*

There's a squashy chair (broken), some tools, and lots of cardboard boxes full of stuff – games and books and old toys.

There's also something big hidden under an old sheet.

MEGAN. Right, first things first, thanks for coming to this EMOOF.

BEN. What you on about: EMOOF?

MEGAN. Emergency Meeting Of Our Friendship. EMOOF. Keep up.

BEN (*smiling*). Right. Soz.

MEGAN. It actually means a lot to me, obvs, so. Yeah.

Also, my mum's got us a box of these to keep us going.

MEGAN *gets a box of broken biscuits out.*

BEN. Nice one.

HOLLY. Yes!

MEGAN. I have actually asked her to stop getting them, get us some just normal biscuits – it's not going in.

HOLLY. These are lovely, Megz.

BEN. They taste of being round yours.

MEGAN. Yeah, cos they're shit.

BEN. It's the only place I've ever had three Jammie Dodgers stuck together to make one Super Dodger.

HOLLY. They're like mutant biscuits. Good mutants. X-Men.

MEGAN. Great.

Right, EMOOF.

Any questions before we start?

BEN. How come we're in your shed?

MEGAN. Tell you in a minute.

HOLLY. Um.

MEGAN. Holly.

HOLLY. What's under there?

MEGAN. Tell you in a minute. I know it sounds daft but I need to do like a big introduction then I'm thinking sort of: reveal.

BEN. Come on then.

MEGAN. Come on then what?

BEN. Reveal!

MEGAN. Right. So.

We've finished, is the thing. School's done, school's over. And looking back, probably, it could've gone better. For all of us. Mainly Ben.

BEN. Cheers.

MEGAN. Like I'm kind of amazed you haven't just put all your revision notes in a massive pile, set fire to them, danced round with a big stick like stabbing them, telling them to fuck off.

BEN. They're just in the recycling.

HOLLY. Already?

MEGAN. So at first I was thinking like: shit. We've basically failed school.

HOLLY. Won't've failed, just –

MEGAN. I don't mean we've failed our GCSEs – well, maybe Ben has actually, some of the stuff you were coming out with, honestly. Science was a disaster. I mean I'm not exactly Einstein but you have seriously misunderstood the carbon cycle.

HOLLY. Megan.

MEGAN. It's alright, I've googled what he can do instead of A levels – it's called an NVQ, Ben. Think you'd really enjoy it.

BEN. Right. Cheers.

HOLLY *gives* MEGAN *a look.*

MEGAN. What?

What?

BEN. I think what Holly's trying to say, with her eyes is: stop going on about how I've probably failed, just leave it as like the elephant in the room, we all know it's there, that's fine, I love elephants, just tell us what's under the sheet.

HOLLY. Exactly.

MEGAN. No offence, Ben, but I'm pretty sure you failing your exams is not the elephant in the room, it's just, basically, a fact. I'm pretty sure the elephant in the room is the enormous, life-changing surprise, under that sheet.

BEN. Tell us then.

MEGAN. I'm getting there.

So, I was thinking how school's been like a massive pile of wank. Not cos of the actual school bit, obvs, more just the bit where we've spent all these years being total losers.

HOLLY. We're not that bad.

MEGAN. Look at this.

MEGAN *chucks* HOLLY *her shirt, from the last day of school. It is covered in marker-pen writing, pictures of dicks, etc.*

On the back, Frithy's bit.

HOLLY. He says good luck.

MEGAN. He says Good Luck Mel. Who the fuck's Mel? I was in his form for three years. He thinks I'm called fucking, Mel.

HOLLY. Might be a G? Sort of, a weird G.

BEN. Nah, that's an L.

MEGAN. Exactly. L for Loser. We're losers.

HOLLY. At least he wrote something. No one wrote on mine, really. Hardly anyone. You two and then, Mrs Bishop.

MEGAN. Mrs Bishop wrote on your leaver's shirt? The Head of IT wrote on your leaver's shirt?

HOLLY *nods*.

HOLLY. Drew me a little picture of a USB stick, waving.

BEN. Sweet.

HOLLY. Yeah.

MEGAN. It's tragic.

BEN. Better than what half the people wrote on mine.

MEGAN. See? We're nobodies. Proper, proper nobodies… I'm all fat and, and gobby, you're brainy, weird and brainy and quiet and Ben's like, you know. No offence but you are, you are quite gay.

BEN. I am gay.

MEGAN. Exactly.

BEN. Completely gay. Hundred per cent.

MEGAN. Stop it.

BEN. What?

MEGAN. Going on about it. I'm a hundred per cent fat, I at least talk about other stuff.

HOLLY. You're not a hundred per cent fat.

MEGAN. I'm not being funny, Holly, my BMI's brown. Brown.

The point is: we're never off to be standard cool are we? We're just not. Cos they're all thin and into like business studies and getting Bs and not being a massive poof.

BEN. I'm just normal size.

MEGAN. Cheers, Ben. Rub it in.

BEN. That isn't what –

MEGAN. We're not sporty and we're not, we're not pretty, apart from Holly, but you wear glasses so people don't notice, like in films.

HOLLY. You're pretty.

MEGAN. No one's ever wanked over me.

HOLLY. Megan!

MEGAN. What?

HOLLY. No one's ever –

MEGAN. I'd check in with Robbie Armstrong about that first, Holly. He's got like a list, The Wank Bank. You're number three.

BEN. Number two now actually. Danielle Chapman got demoted. Cos of that rash.

MEGAN. I actually think you should go out with Robbie Armstrong.

HOLLY. I actually think he's a dick.

MEGAN. Oh.

BEN. I actually think he's gay.

HOLLY. Oh.

MEGAN. The point is: we're capital-L losers. Carry on like this, we're losers for ever. And we don't have to be. We just need: a thing.

BEN. What you on about?

MEGAN. A thing. A thing that's like ours. Something dead special. We've got two months before college starts, fresh start, two months to completely one hundred per cent reinvent ourselves. We can get there, September, just sort of crash through the doors like: guys, we're here, we've arrived, we're cool. Which is why I've got you both here for this EMOOF, hear the new plan.

BEN. I actually don't mind being a loser.

MEGAN. Don't shit on the plan, Ben, before we even start.

BEN. I'm not.

MEGAN. You did this about Disneyland, look what happened there.

BEN. Nothing happened. We didn't go.

MEGAN. Exactly. We did not go to Disneyland. Wasn't that fun?

BEN. I just think –

MEGAN. Stop thinking. Now. Seriously. Stop thinking and just, let me tell you the plan. Big reveal. Once you see what's under there you will realise how important it was that I got you here, see with your own eyes what a great idea I've had, you will want to be spending the next two months in this shed, I promise, I just, I know it.

HOLLY. Thing is, Megan.

MEGAN. Oh for –

BEN. Me and Holly have already got stuff we need to be doing. Like, Holly's just got this job, Sainsbury's Local –

MEGAN. Spring Bank or Prinny Ave?

HOLLY. Prinny Ave.

MEGAN. Fancy.

BEN. I'm working at the, at Murreyfield, where my gran was.

MEGAN. As in the old people's home?

BEN. Yeah.

MEGAN. Doing what?

BEN. Well, it's nice actually, mornings I'm just cleaning and that, ordinary stufff.

MEGAN. Clearing up wee.

BEN. But then that's just the early shift. Once we're done, everything's clean, I've set up these activities like, cross stitch, crochet, knitting and that. For the residents. Calling it: crafternoons.

MEGAN. Right, I'm not being funny, Ben, if I ever hear you use the word crafternoon again, I will smack you.

BEN. Wow. Hostile.

MEGAN. Also, that still leaves plenty of time for us to get on with…

HOLLY. With what?

MEGAN smiles, goes over to the surprise thing, covered in a sheet.

She grins.

MEGAN. Think it's time, guys. Big reveal. Maybe start a countdown.

BEN. You could just show us.

MEGAN. Ten, nine, eight…

She gestures for them to join in.

HOLLY. Seven.

BEN *and* HOLLY. Six.

MEGAN. Excitement mounts.

BEN *and* HOLLY. Five, four…

MEGAN. I can feel it. Can you feel it?

BEN *and* HOLLY. Three…

MEGAN. Like a massive great waft of just –

BEN *and* HOLLY. Two.

MEGAN. Dreams and that.

BEN *and* HOLLY. One…

MEGAN. Get ready for your whole lives to completely change for ever.

MEGAN pulls the sheet off to reveal a drum kit.

TA-DAH!

BEN. Oh. My. Flipping –

MEGAN. I know.

She chucks the old sheet to one side.

BEN. These are immense.

MEGAN. I know.

BEN. Can we have a go?

MEGAN. No, no way.

BEN. Oh.

MEGAN. They're just, they're mine. For me.

HOLLY. Show us then. I mean: you show us.

MEGAN. I am showing you. This is what I'm showing you, this.

HOLLY. No I mean show us some like drumming or something.

MEGAN. I can't do that, Holly.

HOLLY. Oh.

MEGAN. On account of, I can't actually play them yet. The drums.

HOLLY. But –

MEGAN. I know. I literally just saw them in the window, the hospice shop, saw them sitting there in the window, twenty quid, the lot, which I actually hung on a couple of days, talked them down to fifteen cos they're quite bulky, the woman in the shop wanted rid. Said people kept just going in, playing them dead loud, it was doing her head in.

BEN. Was it just you though?

MEGAN. What d'you mean?

BEN. Was it just you kept going in, playing them dead loud?

MEGAN. Probably, who gives? Anyway, I was like: fifteen quid, I'm having them. Yoink. Goodbye being a shitty overweight nobody. Hello rhythm.

HOLLY. Hello.

MEGAN. Got them home, which actually took quite a lot of doing, I had to nick a trolley from Aldi, but I thought: it'll be worth it. It'll all be worth it when I get them set up, start bashing out some sweet sweet beats like a fucking, I dunno. Drummer. So I did. Got them back here, just in my room to begin with but then my mum was like: genius idea, Megan, why don't you try putting them in the shed? That way, we won't be disturbing you so much, probably won't even be able to hear you, hardly. And I was like: good call, Wendy. Good call.

BEN. Wendy?

MEGAN. I'm calling her Wendy for a bit, cos I'm mature and that. She's not enjoying it. But I'm just like: Wendy… Anyway, got them in here, cleared like a space and, yeah. That's it. So…

HOLLY. So…?

MEGAN. We're fucking, doing it! Aren't we though? A band! We're doing a band! Fist-bump. Fist-bump.

BEN. What you on about?

HOLLY. Um.

MEGAN. Us three. Me, you, Holly. A proper band. Cos, think about it: we basically are one already. Apart from the music and the instruments and that. But, just need like one each I reckon. I've got, bagsy drums. And actually, Holly – you've got your flute. So: Friday night, back here. You fetch that.

HOLLY. Oh, no.

MEGAN. You, somehow, get something to play, and like learn to play it a bit, I reckon guitar's best. We'll have a first practice – nothing scary just, give it a shake, see how it swings. Suddenly, out of nowhere, we've got a thing.

HOLLY *looks at* BEN, *desperate for him to say no.*

BEN *smiles.*

BEN. Sounds ace.

MEGAN. What?

HOLLY. Ben.

BEN. It does.

MEGAN. Are you not about to tell me loads of like hundreds of thousands of reasons why you can't do that and why we shouldn't be in a band in the first place and – ?

BEN. Thing is, Megz: you're completely right. It'll be fun, won't it?

HOLLY *looks doubtful.*

It will, Holly. Honest.

It's the summer. We're sixteen. Might as well have
a flipping, go.

MEGAN. Did you just say I'm right? Did you hear that, Holly?
Ben just said something I said is, and I quote, 'right'.

BEN. You're always saying stuff. Got to be right sometimes.

MEGAN. Wow, double-edged, I'll ignore it.

HOLLY. I'm not sure it is right actually.

MEGAN. Don't be a knob, Holly.

HOLLY. There's loads of other stuff we could do. Or you
could do.

MEGAN. Why though? This is literally the best idea I've
ever had.

HOLLY. Maybe get a summer job?

MEGAN. No need – my dad's given me an allowance to say
well done for revising.

HOLLY. But…

MEGAN. But what?

HOLLY. I dunno, just…

BEN. We could be immense.

MEGAN. We will be immense.

BEN. Like The Smiths, Belle and Sebastian, Pulp.

   HOLLY *looks lost*.

MEGAN. Taylor Swift.

   Come on, Holly, you like Taylor Swift.

HOLLY. Everyone likes Taylor Swift, she's a phenomenon.

MEGAN. Exactly. So…?

HOLLY. I just, I wasn't thinking I'd really. I mean, thought I'd
just spend my free time this summer sort of, learning code?

MEGAN. You can learn code any time, Holly. You can learn
code when you're dead.

HOLLY. That's not true.

MEGAN. This is the best chance we've got of stuff going well at college, Holly. It just is. I reckon we'll be really good.

BEN. I do actually think we'll be good.

HOLLY *considers*.

HOLLY. Fine.

MEGAN. Fine?

HOLLY. I mean: I'll try it. For a bit.

MEGAN. Wahey! We're doing it! We're really really doing it! We're a band.

She hammers a cymbal with her drumstick.

We need to have a proper practice though, like set a time aside, once a week, that's just for this, Friday nights.

HOLLY. I'm not free Friday nights.

MEGAN. You're definitely free Friday nights, Holly. You don't have a life, none of us do.

HOLLY. Good point.

MEGAN. Biscuit?

BEN *takes one*.

BEN. Band fuel!

HOLLY *takes one*.

HOLLY. They do taste of being in a band.

MEGAN *eats one*.

MEGAN (*pleased*). They really really do.

2.

MEGAN *has made the shed look nicer – scatter cushions,*
a throw.

She is sitting at the drums, impatient.

HOLLY*'s got her flute, and some fairy lights, which she is*
putting up as they talk.

MEGAN. He's chickened out. Must've.

HOLLY. We could start without him?

MEGAN. Yeah I'm sure that'll sound good – a drum kit and
    a flute. We need guitar. It's like glue for musicians, ask
    literally any band. Shall I just go get him?

HOLLY. Has he definitely got a guitar?

MEGAN. I was there, Holly. Volkswagen Martin turns up, to
    go on a date with Ben's mum – I know, gossip – and Ben's
    like being all awkward, so I started telling him, Volkswagen
    Martin, about us lot, Volkswagen Martin goes 'You're in
    a band? That's brilliant!' And I just sort of shrug like: yeah,
    play drums, no biggie. And then he goes 'I've got a guitar,
    Ben! You can have that.'

HOLLY. What did Ben say?

MEGAN *looks a bit unimpressed.*

MEGAN. 'Maybe.'

She eats a biscuit.

HOLLY. Oh.

MEGAN. But then I was like: thank you, Volkswagen Martin,
    Ben would love to borrow your guitar. And then actually it
    went a bit… you know.

HOLLY. What d'you mean?

MEGAN. Well apparently no one calls Volkswagen Martin
    Volkswagen Martin to his face.

HOLLY. Oh.

HOLLY *eats a biscuit.*

MEGAN. I know. So that was a clanger. But the point is, the actual point is Ben's got a guitar, and he knows to bring it. So he better. Fucking.

BEN *arrives*.

Finally!

He hasn't got a guitar.

BEN. I'm late, soz.

MEGAN. Never mind soz. Where is it?

BEN. What?

MEGAN. The guitar, where is it?

BEN. Oh, change of plan – brought this instead.

BEN *gets a recorder out of his pocket. The kind you play at school. It's in three parts.*

MEGAN. What?

BEN *assembles the recorder.*

BEN. Cos you said like, any instrument, anything you can find. Thought it'd sound nice with Holly's flute. Two blowy things. Plus, I can already play it.

BEN *starts to play 'London's Burning'. He struggles.*

Might need work.

MEGAN *watches.*

What?

MEGAN. You know what.

BEN. I just can't.

MEGAN. You just can.

BEN. Feels too weird using his stuff.

MEGAN. Fucking hell, Ben.

BEN. It does.

MEGAN. Cos he's shagging your mum?

HOLLY. Megan.

BEN. Figured it out then.

MEGAN. Just asking.

BEN. I just don't feel ready to sort of, I dunno.

MEGAN. What?

BEN. Borrow his guitar?

MEGAN. He can shag your mum but you don't feel ready to –

BEN. It's weird, I know it's weird.

But him and my mum, right, it is going a bit fast.

Like yesterday they were sitting there watching *Pointless*, and one of the categories was like Mediterranean Islands – suddenly, out of nowhere he's all: 'I know: why don't we go on holiday? All of us?' As in, me and my mum, and then him and, he's got like two lads. One's older, one's younger. And my mum was like: that sounds lovely, Martin. Kiss kiss kiss, more gin. And I don't want to stop them cos she's not had a holiday for, literally, ever, my mum, not since her and my dad… Well. Not since we moved here, I suppose. But then, also, I do want to stop them.

MEGAN. Where is it?

BEN. What?

MEGAN. The guitar! Honestly, 'what?'

BEN. Just in the front room. Being all like: big and. There.

MEGAN. Get it. Go. Now.

BEN *leaves*.

Finally getting somewhere.

HOLLY. Are you sure that's the right thing to do?

MEGAN. Guitar is definitely better. It just is.

HOLLY. But if Ben's worried about sort of –

MEGAN. That's why he needs the guitar. Cos he can play his way through it, can't he? Through the worries, guitar his way through. That's what all the guitarists do.

HOLLY. Like who?

MEGAN. Just, you know. All of them. It's a really good plan.

HOLLY turns the fairy lights on. They look lovely.

Stunning.

HOLLY. My gran got me them, for my birthday sort of thing.

MEGAN. Absolutely stunning. They are.

HOLLY smiles.

HOLLY. Thought it'd look a bit more band-y.

MEGAN. Definitely band-y. Speaking of which, I'm literally ready to let rip.

She bangs some drums hard.

Think I might've been born to drum.

HOLLY. Not sure I'm born to flute.

MEGAN. Well you better up your game cos I've been practising loads, I won't be holding back. You can't stop the beat, Holly.

MEGAN starts drumming.

HOLLY. Wow.

MEGAN. Can't stop it. It's irresistible. Like Pringles.

HOLLY stands there a bit awkward.

Irresistible. Holly.

HOLLY is still standing still.

Right that's it, I'm stopping, I'm stopping the beat.

MEGAN stops drumming.

What is going on here?

HOLLY. What d'you mean?

MEGAN. The beat's there, the beat's strong, you're resisting it. In quite a stubborn way.

HOLLY. I don't…

MEGAN. I've let you in the band, with your flute, which I'll be honest was a tough call. Now you're just standing round like a lemon not feeling the beat. You've got to let it in.

HOLLY. Let what in?

MEGAN. Fuck's sake, Holly, the beat. These, what are these?

HOLLY. Um. Shoulders?

MEGAN. At the moment, shoulders. Let the beat in, they're like, I dunno. Rhythm... wings.

HOLLY. Is that a thing?

MEGAN. Let the beat in. Find out.

HOLLY. I don't think I know how to let the beat in.

MEGAN. Understatement.

HOLLY. It's not really a flute thing. I just do flute. And computers.

MEGAN. Okay, how do we do this, how do we do this?

Do you think you might be able to hit this drum, just hit it, with this? Like:

MEGAN *hits a drum.*

And then every fourth beat you hit this one as well.

MEGAN *demonstrates a very simple beat.*

It's really hard.

HOLLY. I'll try.

HOLLY *does. Easily.*

MEGAN. And keep going, keep going.

MEGAN *starts to feel it. She starts to move.*

So like, start with maybe...

MEGAN*'s shoulders move to the beat. She also sort of grunts a tune.*

Just, letting it in. Simple. And then sort of: hips and all.

MEGAN*'s hips join in.*

Arms if you like. Nothing too weird just, bit floppy or
something. And then just, add a few bits of your own like:

An arm.

Didn't see that coming.

A leg.

What's that leg?

A move, a genuine move. Your go.

HOLLY *stops drumming.*

HOLLY. Is there any way I can say no?

MEGAN. No.

HOLLY. Thing is: I've actually, I've got quite bad period pain.

MEGAN. It's not PE, Holly. You can't get a note off your mum.

HOLLY. I just –

MEGAN. Dance.

MEGAN *starts to drum.*

Honestly, Holly, learn to dance, your life is better straight
away. No one's ever sad they got the hang of dancing. Billy
Elliot. Beyoncé. Shoulders.

HOLLY *moves her shoulders self-consciously.*

Looser, looser. Go big.

HOLLY. I can't.

MEGAN. Course you can. Go for it!

HOLLY *goes a bit bigger.*

Better. More hips.

HOLLY *tries.*

HOLLY. Megan, I feel like an absolute –

MEGAN. You look immense. Shake it! Shake it! Seriously.

HOLLY. I've never shaken anything in my life.

MEGAN. Now's your chance. Come on, admit it, you're
    enjoying this. You are though. You are.

HOLLY. I'm not not enjoying it. I guess.

MEGAN. Don't stop then. Arms, do some arms.

> HOLLY *starts to laugh.* MEGAN *cheers.* HOLLY *wiggles
> her bum.*

Oh em gee, Holly. Those hips do not lie.

They both get the giggles.

> BEN *comes in with his guitar.* HOLLY *is suddenly
> embarrassed.* MEGAN *is still drumming.*

BEN *grins.*

BEN. What's all this?

HOLLY. Nothing.

BEN. Don't stop!

MEGAN. Get dancing then. Both of you.

> BEN *grabs* HOLLY*'s hand, and gets her dancing again. It is
> really goofy and joyful. They get the giggles, and collapse in
> a heap, laughing.*

See? Fun. I told you.

BEN. It is actually fun.

MEGAN. This is what I'm saying. And we can make everyone
    who's listening, listening to us play, make them want to get
    up and all, get up and dance.

BEN. I can't play anything, Megan. I can't play G.

MEGAN. At the moment but...

> Thing is: I've got this thing right, got this thing in my head,
> can't stop thinking... Where we're just on stage, on an actual
> stage, about to start. Everyone's looking at us, dead quiet. No
> one's expecting anything. And then we start to play and it's
> got, bit of a beat, people are like: decent, bit of a beat. It's
> getting them. And the guitar's sort of fine, nothing flash but
> it's something to start with, and then there's just some words –

HOLLY. Who's doing words?

MEGAN. Stop freaking out, we'll sort it. Also: flute. We look up, they're like, they're on their feet, just properly dancing, cos of us. And there's like people drinking, crowd-surfing, recording it on their phones to put on YouTube and that, and like massive speakers and lights, bright bright lights. That's what I'm picturing. That's what I just keep thinking about.

A football smacks against the shed. Everyone jumps.

BEN. Crikey.

MEGAN. Ben, I really think it's time you learned to swear.

HOLLY. What was that?

MEGAN. Nowt, it's fine, ignore it.

The ball smacks the shed again. HOLLY *and* BEN *flinch. Some lads laugh.*

BEN. Megan, really, what's – ?

MEGAN. Next-door Darren, isn't it?

HOLLY. Oh.

MEGAN. Thinks he's the shit cos he's doing a Young Apprenticeship.

BEN. In what?

MEGAN. Being a dick.

HOLLY. I think it's transport.

MEGAN. He'll stop now.

A moment.

Must've seen us in here, thought like: now's my chance. Now's my chance to be even more of a wanker than usual.

HOLLY. He can't do that. You should tell someone.

MEGAN *shrugs.*

MEGAN. Been like this for ages. Keeps shouting stuff out the window about how I'm like a whale and a heifer and that. Calling me Thunderer.

HOLLY. Poor Megz.

MEGAN. Football's a new development. Cocky shit.

HOLLY. Are you okay?

MEGAN. Reckon he fancies me. Honestly, he never did any of this before I had tits. I used to go round his for Angel Delight. Butterscotch.

HOLLY. Maybe we should practise somewhere else?

MEGAN. Are you kidding? I've spent ages making it decent in here.

BEN. It is lovely.

It isn't.

MEGAN. Next-door Darren can fuck off. We're not scared.

HOLLY. I am a bit scared.

MEGAN. You're not you just think you are.

HOLLY. No I actually am.

MEGAN. Just think about the music, Holly. Be worth it, I promise. Can't let a few knobheads put you off the music. Miley Cyrus didn't. Are you playing this guitar or what?

BEN. I can't.

MEGAN. It's not for show.

BEN. I know but –

BEN *picks it up.*

Think my fingers aren't strong enough or something. I do a chord but…

He plays it.

Comes out fuzzy.

MEGAN. You're not pressing hard enough.

BEN. That's what I mean though, my fingers –

MEGAN. Press harder.

BEN. I can't it's, Martin was saying –

MEGAN. Who's Martin?

HOLLY. Volkswagen Martin.

BEN. We're not calling him that any more.

HOLLY *smiles*. MEGAN *laughs*.

Martin says it takes a bit of time, the skin on your fingers gets little pads, thicker than normal skin, so it doesn't hurt as much.

What?

MEGAN. Nowt. Just thinking, what we can do while we're waiting for the skin on your fingers to get little pads so it doesn't hurt as much.

BEN *laughs*.

BEN. No you're right, I asked for that.

MEGAN *looks grumpy, gets another broken biscuit*.

MEGAN. Right, everyone get one of these.

BEN *and* HOLLY *get a biscuit*.

And then I think we should all swear on the biscuit that next week we'll have a song to play.

BEN. What?

MEGAN. Promise. Promise on the biscuit.

HOLLY. Is that a thing?

MEGAN. Broken biscuits have magical properties. That's why they're not ordinary shapes.

HOLLY. Like X-Men.

MEGAN. If you like.

She holds up a biscuit.

Promise.

BEN. Okay.

MEGAN. On the biscuit. Say I promise on the biscuit next week we'll have a song to play.

BEN. I promise on the biscuit next week we'll have a song
to play.

MEGAN. Holly.

HOLLY. Yep, what Ben said.

MEGAN. Now eat the biscuit.

They all eat their biscuits.

There. Sorted. Can't wait.

3.

MEGAN *is moving stuff around.*

HOLLY *is looking at her laptop.* BEN *is setting up a mic.*

MEGAN *goes through some boxes. She finds a few toys, and
sets some up in a row in front of* BEN *and* HOLLY.

BEN. What's going on?

MEGAN *gestures at the toys,*

MEGAN. Audience.

BEN. Tickle Me Elmo's in the audience?

MEGAN. Yeah. No pressure.

She's sitting comfortably.

Ready. Hang on.

She gets the box of biscuits.

Ready.

BEN. Okay.

BEN *taps the mic.*

Martin says we can have this to keep –

MEGAN. Yes!

BEN. And he has been trying to teach me stuff on guitar but so far I've only got one chord.

BEN *demonstrates*.

MEGAN. Wow.

BEN. So I thought I'd sort of strum that sometimes, while we're singing, but then also, we've got a surprise for you...

MEGAN. If it is that fucking recorder –

HOLLY. It's not the recorder it's, well, um, I had a look at the, it's just like standard software, like garage band or whatever and it's actually, cos we were struggling a bit, playing the, the music –

BEN. I was.

HOLLY. So then we thought: let's try programming some cool sort of, well, sounds I suppose into, yeah, and just like see what happens, so I did, and...

MEGAN. So you've learned a song but you're not actually playing it?

HOLLY. Playing it on this.

HOLLY *points to the laptop*.

BEN. Holly might flute a bit.

HOLLY. And I brought speakers, so...

MEGAN *is absolutely unimpressed*.

MEGAN. Right.

A moment.

BEN. Um. Shall we just...?

HOLLY *gives* BEN *a thumbs up, and presses a button on her laptop*.

It starts to play the music she's programmed.

BEN *starts to sing the first verse of 'Mis-Shapes' by Pulp.*

HOLLY *points at* MEGAN*'s broken biscuits, as the song mentions them.* MEGAN *does not smile.*

HOLLY *presses another button. The sound changes.* BEN *continues to sing. When he gets to the chorus,* HOLLY *joins in with her flute, dead simple.* BEN *continues singing to the end of the chorus,* HOLLY *joining in with some 'Oh oh oh la la la's.*

MEGAN *isn't happy.* HOLLY *presses a button and stops the music.*

Not joining in then?

MEGAN. Give. Me. Strength.

BEN. Like I know I'm not much of a singer, I know that needs work, and obviously, well, the guitar – underwhelming – but all Holly's stuff, it's immense.

MEGAN. It was shit.

BEN. That's not fair, Holly spent ages –

MEGAN. Holly spends ages doing everything, Holly spends ages catching fucking, Pokémon, doesn't mean we all need to hear about it. No offence.

HOLLY. I am a bit offended.

MEGAN. That's not the thing though. The thing is I didn't let you in my band so you could sing along to Holly pressing buttons.

BEN. I just can't play the guitar yet.

MEGAN. Well learn. And learn something that isn't some fucking, song about being losers, that no one's heard of, from like the fifties.

BEN. Nineties.

MEGAN. It's the same thing.

HOLLY. I like it.

MEGAN. Fuck's sake.

BEN. I just thought cos, it says about broken biscuits and that.

MEGAN. Exactly.

BEN. You love broken biscuits.

MEGAN. No. I don't. I mean, I'll eat them, yes, once they're open but they're not... I dunno. Think we should probably aim a bit higher, song-wise. For example, we should only do songs we've written ourself.

BEN. We haven't written any songs.

MEGAN. Yeah we should start.

HOLLY. I'm not sure I can sort of –

MEGAN. You definitely can. You just have to write about important stuff, then make it catchy. Piece of piss.

HOLLY. I really don't think –

MEGAN. The only way we'll figure out how to do it is if we do it.

On actual instruments.

HOLLY. I thought it sounded alright.

MEGAN. It's pretend music, Holly. It sounds pretend.

HOLLY. It sounds electronic, it's still sort of, like lots of bands kind of –

MEGAN. Real bands hit stuff. And sing stuff. And strum stuff. And maybe blow stuff, sometimes. They don't programme stuff. Geeks programme stuff.

HOLLY *blinks*.

She closes her laptop.

We need a name and all. I'll set up a WhatsApp group: Band Names.

We have to crack on cos...

MEGAN *goes to pick something up from by the drum kit. A bit of paper. She waves it about.*

HOLLY. What's going on?

MEGAN. Did you not see it? When you got the stuff through for college?

HOLLY. I daren't even open the envelope, in case I jinx it, and fail all my GCSEs, and I can't go.

MEGAN. You won't fail your GCSEs, Holly. That's Ben.

HOLLY. Megan.

BEN. It's funny cos it's true.

MEGAN. Bet you've still looked though.

BEN. At what?

MEGAN. At all the stuff that came through from sixth form. They posted it, like a welcome pack.

BEN. Oh, I haven't registered yet.

MEGAN. What?

BEN. Yeah, I had a chat with my mum, she said keep my options open a bit, for now.

MEGAN. Right: one. That is mental, what else are you off to do? Get a job? Lol.

BEN. I've got a job.

MEGAN. Or like, go somewhere else, without us, where you've got no mates and you have to do all your coming out again, and they won't be as open-minded as me and Holly? Good one.

Get signed up tonight, they'll send you the brochure. Plus, the first newsletter.

MEGAN *waves the newsletter.*

BEN. Why are you obsessed with the newsletter?

MEGAN. Because, band, the newsletter contains news. Big news. Band news.

HOLLY. What d'you mean?

MEGAN. The first week of term, the first Friday night, they're doing: Battle of the Bands! In like the sports hall.

HOLLY. Oh.

MEGAN. I know.

BEN. Cool.

MEGAN. Think it's a bit more than cool, Ben.

BEN. We can go get some ideas.

MEGAN. We can go one better than that...

BEN. What d'you mean?

MEGAN. I've signed us up, haven't I? Yes. I bloody have.

HOLLY. You've done what?

MEGAN. Signed us up! We are going to have our first gig in exactly nine weeks.

I've made us a chart to count down.

MEGAN *puts a big chart on the shed wall. It says: 'Nine Weeks To Go!'*

What?

BEN. Are you missing school a bit, Megz? Missing having a timetable and that?

MEGAN. I do not thrive without structure.

And I'm not listening to anyone saying no or anyone being knobby, we're doing it, end of. We just need a name, a song, and it was a tenner to guarantee your place but it's for charity so it's okay, but you do both owe me three pounds thirty-three. Bring it next Friday. Deal? Deal.

4.

The chart says: 'Eight Weeks To Go!'

MEGAN *goes into the shed.* HOLLY *and* BEN *are waiting for her.* BEN*'s got his guitar ready.*

MEGAN. Argh! Shit!

HOLLY. Hiya.

MEGAN. Fuck are you – ? Scared the shit out of me.

BEN. We wanted to surprise you.

HOLLY. We've been here like twenty minutes.

MEGAN. Wow. Commitment.

BEN. Just sit down, sit down.

> MEGAN *sits down.*

> Ready?

HOLLY. Bit nervous.

BEN. Be fine.

MEGAN. Not being funny, I've just nearly shat myself coming in here with you two standing there so don't give me any bullshit about being nervous. Whatever you're off to do, fucking… What?

BEN. Ready?

> HOLLY *nods.*

> Two, three, four.

> BEN *plays his guitar.* HOLLY*, shyly, sings.*

HOLLY.
> I work Saturday all day and Thursday night
> And Saturday all day is just alright
> But Thursday night is special, I work from four till ten
> This lad comes in at half-six, buys a Snickers, leaves again
> He's always in a woolly hat, he always picks my checkout
> Near the lottery
> I don't talk to him.

MEGAN *can hardly contain her excitement. She makes a
giddy noise.* BEN *looks at her to be quiet. She has to stuff
the sleeve of her jumper into her mouth.*

> Someone said his name, I think it's Dean
> He is the fittest lad I've ever seen
> He's stood there telling jokes, I'm just blushing at the till
> I'd really like to talk to him, maybe one day I will
> Our fingertips touch when I'm passing him his change
> It's usually twenty-one pee.
> He never wants his receipt.

BEN. Slightly different tune.

HOLLY.
> Mostly I just smile and that is fine
> My mum says there's no hurry, take your time
> He doesn't know my name yet, probably thinks I'm
>   called Marie
> Cos this was her job first and then they gave her badge
>   to me
> The manager said that it wasn't worth making a new one
>   just in case I left.

That's the end.

They stop.

BEN. Um. That is the end.

MEGAN *jumps up and down.*

MEGAN. So much to say.

> One: that was immense, how the fuck did you just…? I mean
> I know I said we were a band but like, I only said it a
> fortnight ago, and I was kind of thinking we probably
> weren't really. Now though: we actually are. You can sing!
> Who knew? And you – what are these? I'll tell you what:
> magic fingers. Since when can you play chords?

BEN *shrugs.*

BEN. I got the hang of G.

MEGAN. And you bloody, writing a song! Where did that
    come from?

HOLLY. I just, well, I googled How To Write A Song. There was this article online called like How To Write A Song, talked you through each step and that. Writing a song. So then I just sort of, yeah. Wrote a song. Half a song. There's meant to be two more verses but I just, I ran out of steam.

MEGAN. Yeah.

BEN. Still though: song.

MEGAN. Well, two more verses, then it's a song. And also, just so you know, just so we're absolutely clear on this: you have to ask him out.

HOLLY. What you on about?

MEGAN. Dean. Fit name, by the way. Has he got a tattoo?

HOLLY. No.

MEGAN. Not to worry. He could get one.

HOLLY. I don't like tattoos.

MEGAN. Well you're wrong but anyway. Can we try it again with drumming?

HOLLY. Do we have to?

MEGAN. Yes we're a band.

HOLLY. What if someone else sings it?

MEGAN. I'm drumming. And Ben can't sing it, it'll sound properly gay.

BEN *and* HOLLY *look at* MEGAN.

Which would be fine, obvs.

BEN *laughs*.

Except it's your song.

HOLLY. What if I just did the same tune but on the flute?

BEN. Like an instrumental.

MEGAN. Thanks, Ben, I did understand it.

BEN. Soz.

MEGAN. Might work, I dunno. Worth a try. You start, I'll just like join in.

BEN. Okay. Two, three, four…

> BEN *strums*. MEGAN *is listening*.

> HOLLY *joins in with the flute*.

> MEGAN *is moving her head*.

> You can start.

MEGAN. I'm just feeling it first, feeling my way. It's like a drummer thing.

> MEGAN *hits a drum. Once*.

BEN. Is that it?

> HOLLY *gets the giggles*.

MEGAN. Something funny, Holly?

HOLLY. Sorry, no, hang on, back on track, back on track.

> *They carry on*. MEGAN *joins in. Very gradually*.

BEN. Sounding good, Megz.

> MEGAN *is really concentrating*.

> Bit louder maybe. And maybe, more than just the one drum.

MEGAN. Fuck off, three-chords, I'm concentrating.

> *A bit more*.

BEN. And then this is the last bit now.

> BEN *and* HOLLY *make it really obvious when to stop*. MEGAN *carries on a bit. Then she stops*.

HOLLY. What d'you think?

MEGAN. I think we have a lot of practising to do. Also: still need a name. There's been a disappointing lack of interest in my Band Names WhatsApp group chat but it is actually quite important. I'll get my pen.

BEN. Why?

MEGAN. You write it on the drum, the big one.

HOLLY. Bass.

MEGAN. Here we go. Strap in. Names.

> MEGAN *is poised by the bass drum, with a big pen, ready to name the band*.

BEN. Holly?

> BEN *grabs a broken biscuit*.

MEGAN. Hit me.

HOLLY. Okay. Right. Um.

> Well I was just thinking about like, I dunno like, next year and that, what we'll be doing next year, hopefully, at college, and I was thinking sort of the two things I'll be doing is sort of hanging out with you two, the band and that, and then, fingers crossed, quite a lot of IT, computers, electronics et cetera so, I just thought, combine the two, maybe we could be called like: The Gigabytes?

MEGAN. Are you serious? The Gigabytes.

HOLLY. I just thought like: Gig. Abytes.

MEGAN. Wow.

HOLLY. Never mind.

BEN. I'd buy their album.

MEGAN. Not being funny, Ben – you bought One Direction's album.

BEN. For you. Cos you asked.

MEGAN. The point of this band's to be cool though.

HOLLY. I think it's cool. And, not just me, other people, you know, other geeks are sort of. There's quite a lot of geeks. Sixth-form geeks. Hopefully. Lots of people would like it, sort of.

MEGAN. Shit people though, the wrong people.

> HOLLY *looks a bit wounded*.

HOLLY. Your go then.

MEGAN. Well. How about – ready? Hang on…

Little drum roll.

Vom.

BEN. Vom?

MEGAN. Yeah like, you know: Vom.

BEN. Megan, that is horrible.

HOLLY. Really horrible.

MEGAN. Maybe we're horrible though.

BEN. We're dead nice. It's like our thing.

MEGAN *huffs.* BEN *takes a deep breath.*

My go then.

BEN *smiles.*

Number-one favourite: Unicorn Onesie.

MEGAN. You bastard.

HOLLY. What?

MEGAN. Promised me, promised me you wouldn't say anything about that. It was one time, I was watching *Gogglebox.*

BEN. I haven't said anything.

MEGAN. No you're just banging on we should tell everyone about, name the sodding band after my unicorn onesie.

BEN. Never said it was your unicorn onesie.

A moment.

MEGAN. Good. Cos I haven't got one.

BEN. Nice save.

HOLLY. You hate onesies.

MEGAN. Exactly. End of.

HOLLY. Megan.

MEGAN. End. Of.

> BEN *smiles at* HOLLY.

> Any others?

BEN. I thought maybe: Racist Uncle?

MEGAN. Are these all just based on my life?

BEN. Is that not okay?

MEGAN. No, course Ben, it's fine.

BEN. Cool.

MEGAN. I'll go next. What about: Ben's A Massive Dick.

HOLLY. It's not super catchy.

> MEGAN *gets a broken biscuit.*

> *She eats it, sadly.*

> HOLLY *and* BEN *exchange a look.*

> You alright, Megz?

MEGAN. Course I'm not fucking alright. We've got eight weeks till we're in front of everyone in sixth form battling bands, we've got three verses of one song and no sodding name. Course I'm not alright.

BEN. We'll do better next week. We will.

MEGAN. I fucking hope so.

BEN. It's just fun, Megz.

MEGAN. It is for you two. You've got bloody, tons of other stuff going on. Murreyfield. Sainsbury's Local. Volkswagen Martin.

BEN. That's more my mum, really. I'm just like a third wheel, wishing they'd slow down a bit.

MEGAN. Learning code.

HOLLY. We can learn it together.

MEGAN. You're alright. I just want you to get that like, this is my thing. This matters. Cos, you know, next year is not going to be easy, is it? Like at all.

BEN. Be alright.

HOLLY. We managed school.

MEGAN. Sort of. I mean we got through it. Just about.

HOLLY. Exactly.

MEGAN. I want to do more than just get through stuff though. I want to like, flipping, I dunno. Take off a bit. Fucking, jump and just… That's what this'll be. If we do it right, put the time in and, really do it. That's what I'm trying to sort of… Yeah.

HOLLY. Maybe you could write a song?

MEGAN *thinks*.

MEGAN. Yeah that is a good plan actually.

I'll get on it.

5.

The chart says: 'Seven Weeks To Go!'

They are all in the shed.

MEGAN. I've got lyrics, haven't got any music.

She takes a folded-up scrap of paper out of her pocket.

BEN. We'll just like, jam.

MEGAN. Fucking hell.

BEN. What?

MEGAN. You have never sounded like more of a wanker. Jam?

BEN. That's what it's called.

MEGAN. That was actually worse than crafternoons. Like a new low.

HOLLY. Shall we get going? I can just mess about a bit on this.

HOLLY*'s got her flute ready.*

BEN. I'll just do a classic two-chord thing. You can sing whatever you like, it'll work.

MEGAN. I want to sing this.

MEGAN *shakes her scrap of paper.*

BEN. I just mean: whatever tune feels right sort of thing. Find a tune, go with it. For now.

MEGAN. Okay.

And I want you two to listen and sort of take it in, the words, cos I actually think it's got quite an important message for us, for next year, and maybe I have been a bit not clear about it. Or maybe you're just not getting it properly, I dunno. One of the two.

BEN. Okay.

MEGAN. Just make it up as I go along sort of thing?

MEGAN*'s still grumpy.*

Like what?

BEN *shrugs.*

MEGAN *counts them in.*

One, two. One two three four.

She sings.

BEN *plays.*

> We dance we sing
> We do cool stuff
> For example, MDMA
> We get tops from Topshop
> We only drink vodka
> People always say
> We're cool
> We're really cool
> We're in a band

BEN. Sounds nice.

MEGAN. Repeat.

BEN *nods*.

> We're cool
> We're really cool
> We're in a band

HOLLY. We're getting the hang of it.

MEGAN. There's another verse:

> School is for losers
> Exams are shit
> We didn't even try
> We just do stuff
> Like house parties
> We never cry

Join in, Holly.

> We're cool
> We're really cool
> We're in a band.

HOLLY *harmonises a bit*.

MEGAN *and* HOLLY.
> We're cool
> We're really cool
> We're in a band.

MEGAN. That's it, that's what I've got.

HOLLY *and* BEN *stop playing*.

Don't be too quick saying well done and that will you?

HOLLY. Oh well done.

BEN. Yeah, course, nice one.

MEGAN. What?

BEN. Nowt just, lots to think about.

MEGAN. Cos you think it's shit? Cheers.

BEN. Don't be daft.

HOLLY. How could it be shit?

MEGAN. There's still like music stuff we need to, it's, you can't just get it right first time when you don't know what you're doing, music-wise.

BEN. Course.

MEGAN. But like the words are… Yeah. That's what next year'll be like.

HOLLY. Do you think?

MEGAN. Definitely.

BEN. Really though?

MEGAN. Definitely. What?

BEN *shrugs*.

BEN. Just, it's not very us.

MEGAN. It's not very us at the moment. It's us next year, sort of, louder and, confidenter, more confident, just like asking lads out, not going on about jam all the time.

BEN. I didn't mean actual jam.

MEGAN. We should try it again. Now we've got a tune sorted. Holly do backing vocals again, I liked that. It's a good sound.

HOLLY. Okay.

BEN *starts to play*.

MEGAN *starts to drum. And sing*.

MEGAN.
We dance we sing
We do cool stuff
For example, MDMA.

HOLLY. Can I just, um –

Everyone stops.

What does it mean: MDMA?

MEGAN. You're actually kidding?

HOLLY *shakes her head*.

Oh. Em. Gee.

HOLLY. I don't…

MEGAN *laughs*.

What?

MEGAN. Nowt, nothing. I mean: sometimes I forget why we're such losers, and then stuff like this happens and I'm just like: yeah.

BEN. It's drugs.

HOLLY. Oh.

BEN. Like ecstasy, I think, except it's powdery. And you just like, I dunno…

MEGAN. You two literally sound like old women.

BEN. I like old women.

MEGAN. It wasn't a compliment.

HOLLY. Just don't really know about drugs, so…

BEN. None of us do.

MEGAN. Well I do but, whatever.

BEN. Really?

MEGAN. My brother and his mates, they're always going on about all the stuff they've done. Like proper cool stuff. Ketamin. Everything. And then us three are just sort of sat here in a shed.

BEN. You made us sit in the shed.

MEGAN. I thought it might inspire you to be a bit less geeky. Apparently not. Apparently you just want to spend your whole summer going on about old women and being shit band members.

BEN. Cheers, Megz. That's encouraging.

MEGAN. I'll be encouraging when you stop being shit.

HOLLY. Are we shit?

MEGAN. We can't even think of a band name.

BEN. I thought of one.

MEGAN. What?

BEN. Hummus. Hummus and the Pitta Breads.

HOLLY. I love hummus!

BEN (*to* MEGAN). You'd be hummus, obvs. We'd be the pitta breads.

MEGAN. I'm not naming our band after a dip.

Some eggs hit the side of the shed.

HOLLY *and* BEN *jump.*

BEN. Is that – ?

MEGAN. Eggs. He's chucking eggs now and all.

BEN. Crikey.

MEGAN *looks at* BEN.

What?

MEGAN. I really wish you'd swear.

BEN. I'm not going to swear.

MEGAN. Why not though? It's really fun.

BEN. I just don't like it.

MEGAN *gives* BEN *a look.*

He's the one egging your shed. If you want to have a go at someone, have a go at him.

Or I'll have a go at him if you like.

MEGAN. You'll have a go at Next-door Darren? Right.

BEN. Talk to him anyway.

MEGAN. Yep, okay, you go talk to him, I'll ring you an ambulance.

BEN. I'm not scared of Next-door Darren.

HOLLY. He is quite big, Ben. And like, aggressive.

MEGAN. I reckon he probably swears.

BEN. Funny. Lol.

MEGAN. Can we get back to band planning?

BEN. Why don't you just tell us what you want us to do?

MEGAN. I've been doing that for weeks, Ben, it's not going in.

BEN. Well there's no point us suggesting stuff is there? It's always wrong.

MEGAN. Maybe suggest some stuff that isn't wrong.

BEN. Like what?

MEGAN. I don't know do I?

HOLLY. What if, for next week, me and Ben have a go at sort of, I dunno, sort of imagining what it'll be like when we're in sixth form? If we do that?

MEGAN. As a song?

HOLLY. Exactly. Like this week you did your version and then maybe we should have a go as well.

MEGAN *shrugs.*

MEGAN. If you like.

HOLLY. We'll do that then.

She eats a broken biscuit.

MEGAN. Also, we're running low on these.

HOLLY. Oh no.

MEGAN. But I figured probably you get a discount, Sainsbury's Local.

HOLLY. Oh.

MEGAN. But it doesn't matter if you don't.

HOLLY. No, no, I'll get more.

D'you think he's stopped?

HOLLY *looks, cautiously.*

MEGAN. Probably just run out of eggs.

6.

The chart says: 'Six Weeks To Go!'

Between BEN *and* HOLLY *they are carrying a noticeboard covered in magazine cuttings and two carrier bags full of colourful fabrics and ribbons and clothes and accessories.*

BEN. Can't stay long but –

MEGAN. What? How come?

BEN. Martin stuff but I just, I was excited so…

HOLLY. Ben's literally done a mood board.

MEGAN. Mood board? Fuck off.

> BEN *reveals the mood board.*

BEN. TA-DAH!

> And this is a bag of like ideas. Got paid this morning so, first time, just went sort of fabric mental, fabric mad.

MEGAN. What you on about?

BEN. I was talking to some of the girls, the crafternoon girls.

MEGAN. Not girls, Ben, they're like ninety.

BEN. They were telling me all these cool, all these secret places to get different fabrics and that. I mean, mostly just Hessle Road but. Cos, thing is: if we're off to be a band that's like proper fresh start isn't it? College. No uniform. Proper chance to try new stuff, image-y stuff. For example, I'd like to have a bit more fun with colour.

HOLLY. That's why, the mood board.

MEGAN. It is colourful.

BEN. Figured just: go wild, dream big.

MEGAN. Right.

> HOLLY *looks in the bag. She's pulling out lovely, colourful fabrics, feather boas, clothes.*

HOLLY. Isn't it brilliant?

BEN. Dig in.

MEGAN. No.

> BEN *is clipping something twinkly in his hair.*

> HOLLY *swishes some fabric round her shoulders.*

HOLLY. What d'you reckon?

BEN. You look amazing.

MEGAN. No.

> HOLLY *takes a photo of* BEN *on her phone.*

HOLLY. So pretty.

MEGAN. Stop it. Holly –

> HOLLY *is helping* BEN *to reposition the fascinator.*

HOLLY. What?

MEGAN. He's not a doll. Stop it.

BEN. Just a laugh, Megz.

MEGAN. Not a laugh.

BEN. Just thought it'd be fun to try, try new stuff.

MEGAN. Won't be that much fun when we're scraping you into A&E though will it? Cos some dickhead's caught you in a fucking…

> MEGAN *searches for the word.*

…tiara.

BEN. It's a fascinator.

MEGAN. That is not the point. You know that's not the point.

BEN. Loads of people in bands wear stuff that's a bit different. And then everyone thinks it's immense, feels dead inspired, has a go themselves.

MEGAN. Nobody's feeling inspired, Ben. You look – and I'm saying this to be kind – you look like a mess.

> BEN *looks hurt.*

HOLLY. Megan.

MEGAN. A total. Fucking. Mess.

BEN. Yeah I heard you.

He gathers himself.

You try it then.

BEN *unclips the fascinator, holds it out.*

MEGAN. No.

BEN *is still holding it out.*

HOLLY. Does anyone want…?

I brought: new box.

She puts a box of biscuits on the chair.

We've done the song as well. Just, verse each sort of thing.
And a chorus.

MEGAN. Is it as shit as all this?

BEN. Probably.

MEGAN. Great.

HOLLY. Well, we could play it anyway, see what you think.

Ben?

BEN *starts playing.*

I start.

It's about sort of, next year.

We said we'd do it about… Anyway.

BEN *gives* HOLLY *a nod.*

HOLLY *sings.*

    We'll wear cardigans and coloured tights
    And do our collars up just right
    Get glasses with really chunky frames
    I'm already saving up.
    Stay late in the computer lab
    Programming which will be fab

I'll build us some apps or maybe games
Or something.

HOLLY *looks at* BEN. *He joins in.*

HOLLY *and* BEN.
No one will say we're weird
Nobody will call us strange
Or dickheads, or losers
For, for a change.

MEGAN. I mean they will do, but anyway.

HOLLY. What?

MEGAN. Call you dickheads.

HOLLY. Ben's bit.

BEN.
We'll meet up in free periods and sit
And chat, drink lattes, maybe knit
Knit something, a tank top or a jumper
I've got a lot of wool.
And there'll be loads of lads about
And one of them will ask me out
We'll go on dates, we'll both hold hands,
We'll have a go at blowjobs.
La la la
And Megan will also get a boyfriend
Cos she's ace.
La la la la la la la.

HOLLY *and* BEN.
No one will say we're weird
Nobody will call us strange
Or dickheads, or losers
For, for a change.

BEN *stops.*

HOLLY. That's it, that's what we wrote.

MEGAN. Right.

BEN. Thought maybe you could do a verse?

MEGAN. The thing is: I think all this stuff about people not having a go at us, they probably will have a go at us if we're dressed really weird and we're singing songs about computers and knitting and that.

Like people will say you're weird. Cos it is weird.

BEN. Good-weird though.

MEGAN. There's no such thing. Not in sixth form. We're in a band, we should just be singing about doing cool stuff, sex, drugs, rock 'n' roll – normal stuff.

BEN. Is that normal?

MEGAN. Wearing jeans.

BEN. What about eyeliner though? Glitter? Cardigans?

HOLLY. Yeah, cardigans.

MEGAN. Can I just remind you both: we are actually trying to be a cool band, aren't we? They all look the same. You wear jeans that are a bit scruffy, in a cool way, and a T-shirt that says a band you like. That's how people know you're in a band. Also who your influences are.

BEN. Like a uniform.

MEGAN. Exactly.

BEN. Like school.

MEGAN. Like cool school. Like college.

BEN. Right.

MEGAN. So, Ben, you have the ones you like, the miserable ones –

BEN. The Smiths.

MEGAN. Holly can have Arctic Monkeys, cos you saw them last year and it's maybe the only properly cool thing any of us have ever done, ever.

HOLLY. My dad got the tickets.

MEGAN. I'll have The Clash.

BEN. Do you even like The Clash, Megan?

MEGAN. Course I do.

BEN. Name one song by The Clash.

MEGAN. 'Fuck Off'. By The Clash.

A moment.

BEN. I don't think that is a song by The Clash.

HOLLY. I could google.

HOLLY gets her phone out.

MEGAN. Or you could just trust me.

BEN. Or you could google.

HOLLY. No signal.

MEGAN. Shame.

What?

BEN. I dunno, just. This was just meant to be like the beginning. Like a first step sort of thing. By the time September got here I was hoping for full-on sequins, boa, eyelashes, sort of caterpillar-to-butterfly transformation.

MEGAN. What if you were like a butterfly who just wore jeans and a T-shirt? Like a moth?

BEN. Jeans and T-shirts it is then. We'll just wear jeans and T-shirts of bands we say we like, even though, as soon as we're on our own, Bieber's cranked up full blast. Megan.

MEGAN. Leave Justin out of this.

BEN. Gladly.

BEN folds up a bit of fabric, puts it back in the bag.

Thanks for coming, sequins.

HOLLY. You can still, we can still sort of, we can look at –

BEN. It's fine.

He is putting stuff back in the bag.

Stuff's only fun, really, if everyone's up for it.

MEGAN. Exactly.

So. Dean: what's happening?

HOLLY. Don't.

MEGAN. What?

HOLLY. Nothing's happening.

MEGAN. Fucking hell, Holly. Why not?

HOLLY. I just, he came in again and I panicked. Didn't do anything. Twice.

MEGAN. Did you freeze?

HOLLY. I did, I froze. He bought his Snickers. I gave him his change. Didn't even smile.

MEGAN. Holly!

HOLLY. And then this week, he came in again, didn't even look at me. Just went straight to the self-scan.

MEGAN. Ouch. Burn.

HOLLY. I thought, I can't write another verse about not talking to him, I've already done three. So I didn't.

MEGAN. Right, thing is: just forget the song for a minute, forget about the song for a minute. The point of this isn't writing a song.

HOLLY. Thought it was.

MEGAN. The point of this is writing a good song. Which means you can't be thinking about the song till after you've got something to put in the song. Something good. So just: one – go for it, with Dean; two – tell us what happens. Through song.

HOLLY. I can't do it. Like, as it was happening, in the moment, I just got stuck. Didn't say a word. Normally I'd be all 'that's seventy-nine pee please', but he had the cash ready so I couldn't even do that. I just got suddenly really aware I was talking to, to a lad sort of thing.

MEGAN. It is hard.

BEN. I'm a lad. You talk to me.

MEGAN. She means like a laddy lad. Like an actual, you know. Lad. What?

BEN. Cheers.

MEGAN. You in a huff again?

BEN. It is a bit...

MEGAN. This isn't about you, Ben.

BEN. I know but.

MEGAN. Just pop your tiara back on. Lad.

BEN. It's. A fascinator.

MEGAN. Fuck off.

BEN. Is that by The Clash?

MEGAN *laughs*. BEN *spots the time*.

I should go.

HOLLY. Ben, she didn't mean to –

MEGAN. I bloody did.

BEN. No, I know, just Martin's picking me up like five minutes ago.

MEGAN. Give it another half-hour, your mum'll still be attached to his face.

BEN. Mum's not in, she's not coming. Just me and, Martin and. Well. 'The lads.'

HOLLY. Oh.

BEN. Yeah. Pizza. We're bonding apparently. My mum reckons we need to find some sort of common ground.

HOLLY. Good luck.

MEGAN. Maybe wear this?

MEGAN*'s fished a sparkly dress out of* BEN*'s bag of stuff.*

BEN *smiles*.

BEN. They already think it's weird I have Hawaiian pizza. Who knew ham was gay?

MEGAN. I think it's the pineapple.

HOLLY. Ignore her.

BEN *smiles*.

BEN. Can I leave this here? Pick it up next time.

BEN *indicates the mood board and the bag of stuff*.

They might not get it.

MEGAN. Course. Go.

BEN. In a bit.

HOLLY. See you.

MEGAN. Laters.

BEN *leaves*.

MEGAN *looks at the dress in wonder*.

HOLLY. You could try it?

MEGAN *snorts*.

MEGAN. Yeah good one.

HOLLY. You could.

MEGAN. I'd look like a glitter ball. Be better off in my fucking, onesie.

HOLLY. Which you don't own.

MEGAN. Exactly.

HOLLY. Reckon you'd look nice. Pretty.

MEGAN. Think pretty's asking a bit much.

HOLLY. Megz.

MEGAN. To be honest, I would settle for normal. Like: fine. If people just like noticed me enough to remember my name.

HOLLY. That wasn't you, that was him.

MEGAN. Well then. Stick to my jeans.

Anyway, it's you I'm worried about.

HOLLY. Oh. What?

MEGAN. You just, you're trying not to talk about Dean. Which I definitely think is more important right now.

HOLLY. I might just, probably leave it to be honest.

MEGAN. Leave what?

HOLLY. The whole, the Dean thing?

MEGAN. No. No way.

HOLLY. Honestly, it's –

MEGAN. I'm intervening, Holly, right. This is, it's an intervention. One: You definitely like him, and you never like anyone, not even Robbie Armstrong, and he's been, literally –

HOLLY. You said.

MEGAN. But Dean. Dean. Dean's just turning up, in his little hat, telling you jokes and that, buying a Snickers. And you're all like: swoon. Both like each other. It'll probably never be this simple again. Ever. If you don't believe me, watch *Hollyoaks*.

HOLLY. You're alright.

MEGAN. You just need to bloody, talk to him.

HOLLY. Maybe.

MEGAN. What you on about maybe? D'you know what, it probably sounds daft cos I've not exactly, I'm not exactly super-experienced myself, in the love department, but I have been watching my brother shagging his way through the local Tinder community, and d'you know what: you have to show willing. It's fine just being dead shy and that, to begin with, but you have to give them something. Otherwise they get bored, look for someone else.

HOLLY. Not sure I'm quite. I dunno. Could do with a plan really.

MEGAN. The plan is: talk to him. That's it. Next time he comes
     in for his Snickers, just talk to him a little bit.

HOLLY. Do my best.

MEGAN. Promise.

   A moment.

HOLLY. Promise.

   MEGAN *smiles.*

7.

The chart says: 'Five Weeks To Go!'

MEGAN *goes into the shed.* HOLLY *and* BEN *are waiting for
her.* BEN*'s got his guitar ready.*

MEGAN. Argh! Shit!

HOLLY. Surprise.

MEGAN. Again? Fucking hell. You don't learn.

BEN. We don't learn?

MEGAN. What are you doing anyway?

HOLLY. Got another verse.

MEGAN. No. Way. Did you shag him?

HOLLY. Megan.

MEGAN. You've lost your Vs. I thought you looked different.

BEN. Just, sit down, sit down.

   MEGAN *sits down.* BEN *strums.* HOLLY *sings.*

HOLLY.
     I work Saturday all day and Thursday night
     And Saturday all day is just alright
     But Thursday night is special, I work from four till ten

This lad comes in at half-six, buys a Snickers, leaves again
He's always in a woolly hat, he always picks my checkout
Near the lottery.
I don't talk to him.

MEGAN. Shit, Holly – why not?

HOLLY. I just –

BEN. Hang on.

HOLLY.
Someone said his name, I think it's Dean
He is the fittest lad I've ever seen
He's stood there telling jokes, I'm just blushing at the till
I'd really like to talk to him, maybe one day I will
Our fingertips touch when I'm passing him his change
It's usually twenty-one pee.
He never wants his receipt.

MEGAN. This is sounding very familiar.

BEN. Patience.

HOLLY.
Mostly I just smile and that is fine
My mum says there's no hurry, take your time
He doesn't know my name yet, probably thinks I'm
    called Marie
Cos this was her job first and then they gave her badge
    to me
The manager said it wasn't worth making a new one just
    in case
I left.
I haven't left.

(*Whispers*.) This is the new bit.

Tonight though he comes in at half-past six
Grabs himself a Snickers, leans over, grabs a Twix
They're on offer this week, buy one get one free
Says it's fine if I don't want it but he's bought the Twix
    for me
But if I would rather have the Snickers that is fine
He doesn't mind
He likes both.

He's cheeky and he knows it but he's grinning
It feels a little bit like a beginning
I don't know what to say, put his chocolate through the
  checkout
Smile and keep the Twix and then decide to stick my
  neck out
Write my name on his receipt so he can add me if he likes
On Facebook
And he did.

MEGAN *screams*.

MEGAN. Argh! This is so exciting! A hundred per cent song!
About actual cool stuff. Have you been chatting?

HOLLY. Yeah.

MEGAN. Are you meeting up?

HOLLY. Yeah.

MEGAN. In real life? Not at Sainsbury's Local.

HOLLY. In real life.

MEGAN. Fucking hell, can we come?

HOLLY. Um.

BEN. Course we can't.

MEGAN. What if we come in disguise?

HOLLY. He doesn't know you anyway. There'd be no point. In
a disguise.

MEGAN. Oh I want to go on a date.

BEN. Ask someone out then.

MEGAN. No one fancies me. You were my one big hope.

BEN. Soz.

MEGAN. I say big…

BEN. Cheers.

MEGAN. I'm over it anyway. I'm living through Holly. When's
your date?

HOLLY. Tomorrow.

MEGAN. Have you shaved your legs?

HOLLY. Yep.

MEGAN. What about... down there?

HOLLY. We're not having sex, Megan.

MEGAN. What if it just happens?

HOLLY. I don't think it will.

MEGAN. It might do.

HOLLY. We're only looking for Pokémon.

MEGAN. Is that like a code?

HOLLY. No.

MEGAN. Are you sure though?

HOLLY. Dean's not doing that well, in terms of levels. His Pokédex is barren. And I found a load yesterday, on the marina so I said we could maybe, yeah. I dunno.

MEGAN. You're literally playing Pokémon Go on your first date?

HOLLY. Cool eh?

MEGAN. I wouldn't go that far.

HOLLY. And then Dean says maybe we can have like a hot chocolate or an ice cream or something, depending on the weather. I can't wait.

MEGAN. I still think you should be ready.

HOLLY. For what?

MEGAN. For things to get a bit, you know. Steamy.

BEN. Megan.

MEGAN. And always use protection. Always. That's important.

Ben, lend her one of yours.

BEN. What?

MEGAN. One of your johnnies. Condoms.

HOLLY. It's honestly fine.

BEN. I've not got any.

MEGAN. That's a lie.

BEN. It isn't.

MEGAN. School gave you loads. All the lads. When they did the Big Talk. Cooper put one on his head. Fetch them now.

BEN. I can't.

MEGAN. What you on about?

BEN. They're all… gone.

MEGAN. No way.

BEN. What?

MEGAN. You've been having sex?

BEN. No just.

BEN *looks embarrassed*.

Practising.

MEGAN *laughs*.

It's good to get the, get the hang of it. Just in case I ever do have sex. Which I know is unlikely.

MEGAN. You practised putting them on?

BEN *nods*.

Yourself?

BEN *nods*.

How hard can it be?

BEN. There's definitely a knack.

MEGAN. Shit, Holly, have you got the knack?

HOLLY. I'm only having a hot chocolate.

MEGAN. How hot?

HOLLY. Megan, will you stop making it all about sex? I'm really nervous as it is, it is literally the first date I've ever been on, and I do actually like him, I think he's, you know, quite nice so, so it's enough to get my head round without all, you know…

MEGAN. Holly, he asked you out. He's a lad. It probably is about sex.

BEN. Not straight away.

MEGAN. You've not even had sex, you've used up a whole pack of johnnies.

BEN. So?

MEGAN. So how desperate will you be by the time you're on an actual date?

There's no point being all innocent about it, Holly. He wants to find a few bloody Pikachus or whatever, then he wants a shag.

That's lads.

And you might as well, otherwise everyone'll just say you're dead frigid and you might not get another chance. Unless you go to like uni or something. Tenerife.

HOLLY. I'm not sure that is lads, Megan.

MEGAN. Honestly, you should hear my brother going on about it. And he's older.

BEN. Not everyone's like your brother though.

MEGAN. No, you're right actually. They're mostly worse.

BEN. Megan.

MEGAN. I just think you should be ready for –

HOLLY *gathers her stuff, runs out.*

BEN. Are you not going after her?

MEGAN. Why?

BEN. Cos you've really upset her. She's really upset.

MEGAN. If me telling her about it's freaking her out, him
doing it'll –

BEN. He bought her a Twix, Megan. He asked her to help him
look for Pokémon. I don't think it's the same as your
brother's lot.

MEGAN. Just cos he seems –

BEN. Oh for –

MEGAN. What?

BEN. Are you going to check she's alright?

MEGAN. She's fine.

BEN. I'll go then.

MEGAN. What?

BEN. Sometimes, Megan, sometimes you're a massive dick.

BEN *leaves*.

8.

The chart says: 'Four Weeks To Go!'

BEN *and* MEGAN *are in the shed.*

MEGAN. Nice of you to show up, Ben.

BEN. Don't be like this.

MEGAN. I'll be how I like. Friday night, it's band night, nobody's fucking here.

BEN. Wonder why?

MEGAN. Cos you're all being really pathetic.

BEN. Not staying anyway, just.

Left this here, so.

He picks up his guitar.

He's been asking after it. Martin.

MEGAN. Right.

BEN. He's making a massive thing out of taking an interest. Wish he wouldn't.

MEGAN. Tell him to fuck off then.

BEN. I won't, actually.

MEGAN. Why not?

BEN. Well I don't say the eff-word, as a rule. Which you already know.

MEGAN. Don't know why.

BEN. Cos it is pretty much the main feature of my dad, from what I remember. That and leaving. I'm trying to be a better sort of human.

MEGAN. You are a better sort of human.

BEN. Also, I don't really want to be horrible to Martin, cos he's alright and we're off on holiday tomorrow so –

MEGAN. You're what?

BEN *nods*.

BEN. Just for a week. Fishing trip.

MEGAN. You're going fishing? You?

BEN. They've got like a spare rod, apparently. They reckon I'll really enjoy it.

MEGAN. Ben, I'm not being funny but you can't go on holiday next week. Next week is like potentially the most important week of your whole entire life. Apart from Battle of the Bands week, obvs.

BEN *doesn't understand*.

Results. Results day. GCSE results day.

BEN. Oh.

BEN *shrugs*.

School just post them to you anyway, if you're not there. I'm not expecting great things to be honest. Think I like it better not knowing.

MEGAN. But it's like a massive day, everyone'll be there sort of cheering or sobbing into envelopes and that. It's like the end of, dunno. Like the last bit of...

BEN. School. Which I hated.

MEGAN. Thought you'd be there though. You and me and, and Holly.

BEN. Oh. Okay. No. Sorry.

MEGAN. Not speaking to me is she? Probably just with bloody, Dean.

BEN. I doubt it.

MEGAN. Not answering my texts, WhatsApps, ignoring my Snapchats, even though at least one of them was to do with hacktivism, which she loves.

BEN. You should talk to her.

MEGAN. Maybe you could talk to her about results day? Ask her to come with us. Well, with me now I guess.

BEN. I hate being in the middle of stuff.

MEGAN. So there's stuff?

BEN *shrugs*.

BEN. I should go pack anyway.

MEGAN. Ben, you can't go on holiday now.

BEN. Not really a holiday, is it? Catching, killing and gutting fish. In a small boat. With some thugs.

MEGAN. So don't go.

BEN. My mum –

MEGAN. Your mum should know better, she is actually being irresponsible. What if your results are really bad? I say if – when.

BEN. She's not fussed.

MEGAN. What you on about?

BEN. She knows I tried my best, I'm just not exam-y.

Thinks it's more important we all go, have like a really good time together.

MEGAN. Stay here, stay at mine.

BEN. Nah.

MEGAN. We can like band all week, like properly focus and then, Thursday, all go in together, me, you, Holly, be there for opening the envelopes, hugging, handing out tissues and that.

BEN. I can't.

MEGAN. Course you can. Just tell them you're not going.

BEN. I have to go.

Deep breath.

My mum reckons he's the one so. Seems pretty in love and that. And she's sick of our landlord, there's tons of damp, he never does anything about it. And Martin's got a spare room at his so, for me so… So we're moving in. In like three weeks.

MEGAN. You're moving?

BEN. Yeah. To Thorngumbald.

MEGAN. What about college?

BEN. There's a sixth form there. Apparently they've never had a lad doing textiles but, you know.

MEGAN. We'd never had a lad doing textiles.

BEN. Exactly. I'm a maverick.

Or actually I might not do college at all, I might do more care-y stuff, like get better at that. Cos I know it sounds daft but I actually really like it at Murreyfield. I hardly ever mess up, and the oldies sort of, yeah, I dunno. Love me.

MEGAN. Ben, this is actually…

BEN. What?

MEGAN. Well it's a bit of a bombshell.

BEN. I know.

MEGAN. You leave there's no – is there? No band.

BEN. Holly's gone off it anyway. And she's the one who's done a good song.

MEGAN. Mine's alright.

BEN. Maybe.

MEGAN. Fuck off.

BEN *shrugs*.

Bye then. Dick.

A moment.

BEN *doesn't leave*.

BEN. I'm actually not a dick, Megan.

MEGAN. I learned a new beat.

MEGAN *goes to sit down*.

BEN. Megz. Don't be like this.

MEGAN. Here.

She plays it.

She stops.

BEN. Ace.

MEGAN. I'm sorry I called you a dick.

BEN. I'm sorry we're not a band any more.

MEGAN. But we are though. We have to be. It's our big big chance, you can't just, can't both just...

BEN. I am sorry.

MEGAN. So be in the band. Come to college. Don't move house.

BEN. It's not like I want to move house, Megan. This isn't a thing I'm choosing. I mean I haven't slept for three weeks worrying about it, I've got to start at a completely different sixth form, in a new town, literally live in the same house as two teenage lads who drink protein shakes, arm wrestle about who gets the remote while I sit in the corner, quietly embroidering a kimono.

MEGAN. That never happened.

BEN. Tuesday night.

MEGAN *doesn't know what to say.*

MEGAN. How's the kimono?

BEN. Detailed.

The point is: I know it's rubbish to not be here, with you, the band, and I know it's rubbish to not live on our street any more, but it is happening, and I can't do anything about it, so maybe just don't have a massive go at me, cos it's not my fault and I'm trying my best and maybe, maybe you could see how hard it is for me sometimes as well, without me having to spell it out. Maybe you could think about that. Or at least, I dunno, make room for us a bit.

MEGAN. I have made room.

BEN. You haven't.

MEGAN. I've literally provided a shed. It's literally a room.

BEN. And then told us what we can and can't do, what sort of band we have to be, what sort of songs we're meant to like –

MEGAN. I'm trying to help.

BEN. What clothes we're allowed to wear.

MEGAN. I knew it! Ha!

BEN. What?

MEGAN. You're just pissed off cos I said you looked daft in a tiara, cos you did. That's what all this is about – your fucking tiara. What?

BEN *takes a deep breath.*

BEN. Right.

In a minute, I'm off to play you a song right –

MEGAN. You've written a song?

BEN. Yep.

MEGAN. Shit, Ben, this is immense.

BEN. And I, I don't want you to say anything, don't want to talk about it, I never wrote it to play anyone really but I just, I'm playing you it, and then I'm leaving okay?

MEGAN. Okay.

BEN. And I'm off to wear this.

BEN *picks up a sparkly dress out of the bag of stuff, and puts it on.*

MEGAN. Fucking hell, Ben –

BEN. Just: listen.

He picks up the guitar.

He sings.

> I am not a mess
> I'm just a lad
> A lad in a dress
> A glittery dress.

You can take the piss if you must
It's either this or another pair of jeans.

But sometimes it's nice to sparkle
Nice to stick out a bit.
Sometimes I feel like shimmering
Sometimes I just feel shit.

If you want to wear your jeans, wear your jeans
Have a go at eyeliner it's mad
I'll be stood here in my dress
Nevertheless
I'm just a lad
A glittery lad
La la la la.

You can take the piss if you must.
It's either this or just sitting by yourself.

If you want to try and be cool, try and be cool
Have a go at being someone else.

I'll be stood here in my dress
My glittery dress.

Cos sometimes it's nice to sparkle
Nice to stick out a bit.
Sometimes I feel like shimmering
Sometimes I just feel shit.

A moment.

MEGAN. You swore.

BEN. What?

MEGAN. You said shit. Quite a few times. And piss.

BEN. Oh. Yeah.

BEN *puts the guitar away.*

Right. See you then.

MEGAN. Whoa. Hang on.

MEGAN *holds on to* BEN.

BEN. What?

MEGAN. You're not going out like that?

BEN. What d'you mean?

MEGAN. Wearing that?

BEN. Yep.

MEGAN. Get dressed, properly, now.

BEN. But –

MEGAN. Now.

BEN. Why?

MEGAN. Ben, I'm not being funny but if Next-door Darren sees you, or like anyone really, but, he is actually quite hard and he won't have a problem, like he won't start on me or, or Holly cos, you know, but you are technically a lad –

BEN. I am a lad.

MEGAN. Exactly, he will not have any worries about just smacking you, just fucking… Now. Dress off. Now.

BEN. See you, Megan.

BEN *picks up his guitar and leaves.*

9.

The chart says: 'Three Weeks To Go!'

MEGAN *is alone.*

She sits at the drum kit, and plays a simple, loud beat.

She sings.

MEGAN.
>Maths: B.
>English: B.
>English Lit: B.
>Science: Two Bs.
>Geography: C.
>Technology: C.
>French: E.

>I'm not cool
>I've got no mates
>I'm not in a band.

MEGAN *sits, sad.*

She looks at her school shirt, covered in writing.

HOLLY *arrives.*

HOLLY. Oh.

MEGAN. You came?

HOLLY. Um, yeah.

MEGAN. Fucking hell, Holly, you came.

HOLLY. Yep, I just –

MEGAN. I thought you wouldn't come, I didn't think you'd…

HOLLY. Well. I guess. Um.

MEGAN. Well done for yesterday, by the way. Properly though. I couldn't find you to say but. Everyone was going on how well you'd done.

HOLLY. Cheers.

MEGAN. That is a lot of A stars. Like a constellation of A stars.

HOLLY. Oh. Well.

How did, how were yours?

MEGAN. Fine, yeah. Well. Mostly Bs and Cs, and then like an E but sort of who gives a shit about French? *Moi? Non.*

HOLLY *nods.*

Just us then? Flute and drums. Probably be fine to be honest. I'm not sure Ben adds that much really.

HOLLY. Um, actually, I just –

MEGAN. Or drums and singing maybe? Pared-down sound.

HOLLY. Actually, um. I'm not really here for band stuff.

MEGAN. Oh, I thought –

HOLLY. Yeah. Well. I'm more just…

I'm just here because, I thought you'd be in, and.

HOLLY *unplugs the fairy lights, starts to take them down.*

I guess before, when I brought these over before I thought they'd help make the shed look nice, but then now I think I'd rather have them in my room. At home.

MEGAN. Oh.

HOLLY. I would've just left them, got some new ones but they're actually quite expensive, and they were off my gran for my birthday so they're a bit special really.

MEGAN. Course. I mean: yeah.

HOLLY. And then I just thought I'd stop coming round. Any more.

MEGAN. What?

HOLLY. Just think, sort of. Well. Been thinking about all the stuff you said, how going to college is a fresh start and that, and I think, yeah, you're definitely right.

MEGAN. It is a fresh start.

HOLLY. Exactly.

And I think, think maybe my fresh start should be like finding some people to hang out with who are into sort of the same stuff as me, sort of graphic novels, learning code, et cetera.

MEGAN. You will do.

HOLLY. So think that's what I'll do really. Cos. Yeah. Like it hasn't been making me happy really – the band and that – and I just.

A moment.

Anyway, I better –

MEGAN. Don't do this, Holly.

HOLLY. I do think it's the best thing.

MEGAN. Like, even the fairy lights, just taking down the fairy lights –

HOLLY. They are my fairy lights.

MEGAN. That's what I mean though. When you've not been here and I've been sort of, I dunno. Like I keep looking at them and just thinking, probably sounds daft but. That is what you bring to the shed. I mean you literally brought them to the shed, obvs. But then, if I think about sort of what you are like, as a mate… Yeah. Little, twinkly bits of light.

HOLLY. You can get new ones, they're just off the internet.

MEGAN. I know but.

HOLLY. I just, I feel like I should go now.

MEGAN. Is it cos of Dean?

HOLLY. What d'you mean?

MEGAN. Is it cos I said that stuff about Dean? Cos I honestly, like, I keep thinking about it and I just, if I could scrunch all the words back up, sort of shove them back in my mouth, chew them, swallow them, so they didn't come out, that's what I'd do.

HOLLY. Right.

MEGAN. And the daft thing is: probably fine, wasn't it? In the end. Probably just went and found some Pokémon, did you? Had a hot chocolate.

HOLLY. I didn't go, so…

MEGAN. How come?

HOLLY. Just thought: probably not ready to, sort of, so…

MEGAN. Shit, Holly.

HOLLY. No it's fine.

Probably for the best, so…

Focus on college-y stuff for a bit.

MEGAN *looks really sad*.

But I will go now, I think.

MEGAN. I really was trying to help.

HOLLY. Maybe.

MEGAN. I was. I know I went on about being cool and that all the time but –

HOLLY. I don't think being cool's that good, to be honest.

I'm more into sort of figuring out who you are, in yourself, and then just being that.

But sort of more. Being more yourself.

So I'm off to do that, I reckon.

MEGAN. Right.

HOLLY. I better…

HOLLY *leaves*.

MEGAN *pulls the chart saying 'Three Weeks To Go!' down, scrunches it up, and chucks it to one side*.

10.

The drum kit is wrecked.

Someone has sprayed 'LOSERS' on the back wall.

The audience of cuddly toys have been chucked around and some of them ripped apart. The bag of costume ideas is spread all over and torn and trampled on.

BEN *and* HOLLY *stand in the middle of it.*

BEN. It's like a flipping, massacre.

HOLLY. I know.

BEN *picks up Tickle Me Elmo. His head is loose.*

BEN. Like the end of childhood.

HOLLY. Like the end of *Toy Story.*

BEN. Poor Megan.

HOLLY. Where is she?

BEN *shrugs.*

BEN. Dunno.

They both just stand there a moment.

What now?

HOLLY. I guess sort of: clear up?

BEN *picks up a drum. It's broken.*

BEN. Can you remember how they went?

HOLLY *can't.*

BEN *looks at the graffiti.*

D'you think we can scrub that off? Just as sort of a nice gesture or something?

HOLLY. Looks quite permanent.

A moment.

They take everything in.

BEN. It's so sad.

HOLLY. I know.

BEN. Like: give up now, or something.

A moment.

MEGAN *leaps out of a box, in a unicorn onesie.*

MEGAN. AAAARGH!

BEN *and* HOLLY *scream.*

BEN. Fucking hell!

HOLLY. Megan!

MEGAN. You said it, you fucking, said it.

BEN. Scared the shit out of me.

MEGAN. Yes! I knew it!

HOLLY. I actually thought I was going to die.

MEGAN. Was it the onesie? Bet it was. I feel so mythical.

BEN. You had us properly scared.

MEGAN. I know – soz.

I just, I thought of doing it, and then once I'd thought of it,
I sort of had to do it, just one of those things.

BEN. No, I mean: we were worried about you.

MEGAN. How d'you mean?

BEN. Thought your spirit might be crushed.

MEGAN. Fuck off.

I've been hiding in there like an hour and a half just to hear
you scream.

BEN. Your dad never said.

MEGAN. He was in on it. Actually, he was quite encouraging
about the whole thing.

Cos I told him how we'd all sort of, you know, sort of fallen
out and everything.

And he said sometimes a big shock makes you realise what's important and that.

And I guess that Next-door Darren breaking into the shed and wrecking everything, I guess that was like my big shock, and then I thought maybe if I jumped out of a box at you both dressed as a unicorn, maybe that might be your big shock.

HOLLY. It was a shock.

BEN. I feel shocked.

MEGAN. And also maybe if I said that I'm sorry, that might also be a bit of shock.

If I said that I was actually, you know, wrong. About stuff.

BEN *and* HOLLY *look at each other.*

HOLLY. That's quite a big shock.

BEN. Massive.

MEGAN. Good. Job done.

BEN. And it was definitely Next-door Darren?

MEGAN *nods.*

MEGAN. Got pissed with his mates and then…

His mum's been round with him, made him apologise and that, begged us lot not to tell the police cos he'll get kicked off his, they'll stop him being a Young Apprentice.

Turns out he's absolutely desperate to be a Young Apprentice. It actually looked like he'd been crying.

HOLLY. Shit.

MEGAN. I know: pathetic.

HOLLY. So, you're not broken?

MEGAN *shakes her head.*

MEGAN. I'm sort of determined actually.

BEN. Determined to…?

MEGAN. Got a plan.

> But I wanted to run it past you both first, if that's, if that's okay.

> That's why I called another EMOOF.

> But I know it's cheeky, so thanks for coming and that.

> I know you didn't want to.

BEN. We did want to.

HOLLY. Ben came from Thorngumbald. On his bike.

MEGAN. No way.

BEN. Tell us the plan.

> MEGAN *starts to reassemble the drum kit.*

MEGAN. I thought maybe we could just give up on the Battle of the Bands night, at college, cos we sort of have to anyway cos Ben won't be there, and also, not in a bad way, but I do think maybe we're not quite there song-wise.

HOLLY. Okay.

MEGAN. But then I was thinking: we could still be a band, maybe. If you were both... We just need songs. And for Ben to not mind getting on his bike a couple of times a week. You might have to leave your guitar here though, so you won't be able to practise much.

BEN. Martin's got another one anyway.

MEGAN. Martin's a legend.

BEN. Well...

MEGAN. And then I was thinking, once we've had a bit more time and we're ready, once we like all agree that we're ready, maybe we could do an actual real-life gig? Maybe at, d'you know The Sesh? Maybe there. But mostly I just think it would be really lovely if we could keep Friday night as like band night, sort of precious, just us three. And also, yeah. I reckon, um...?

*She gets a chunky marker pen, writes 'BROKEN BISCUITS'
on the bass drum.*

BEN *and* HOLLY *look delighted.*

HOLLY. I'm probably not ever going to be cool.

MEGAN. I know, I know.

BEN. Accidentally cool. Maybe. At best.

MEGAN. What d'you reckon?

BEN *and* HOLLY *look at each other.*

HOLLY. Good plan.

MEGAN. Yeah?

BEN. We were sort of hoping that'd be the plan.

MEGAN. Right.

BEN. Brought this in case.

BEN *gets his dress out of his bag.*

MEGAN. Get it on then.

BEN *puts it on.*

It's been in the wars a bit, but.

She clips the (slightly damaged) fascinator into his hair.

BEN. Really?

MEGAN. Pretty.

HOLLY *puts on a boa and starts picking up the toy
audience.*

HOLLY. Poor Elmo. Poor Furby.

BEN. Buzz Lightyear's seen better days and all.

MEGAN. He'll be right.

BEN *looks at* HOLLY.

BEN. Go on then.

MEGAN. What?

HOLLY. Um, well, actually. Dunno if it's, but, anyway.

We brought you a song.

MEGAN. No way.

BEN. It's your song, just different.

HOLLY. Yeah, you have to join in.

BEN. It's drummy.

MEGAN. Obvs.

HOLLY. And I've done some computer stuff and all, just in case, but it's fine if you'd rather just not have that.

MEGAN. We should definitely have it.

BEN. Phew.

HOLLY. It's weird, cos I was sort of thinking about it and… It's the first time I've, I can sort of see it, in my head, with us lot just. Ben's guitaring and that. In his sequins. You're drumming, in your onesie maybe. And the lights are all flashing, you're smacking the drums like absolutely belting them, cos it's all about the beat really –

MEGAN. It is all about the beat.

MEGAN *starts a beat.*

HOLLY. And you've got, you're strumming a bit like –

BEN *plays his guitar.*

Just dead happy, dead dance-y. Like a bit sort of, you know.

BEN. I know exactly.

MEGAN. And everyone's cheering, cos of your sequins.

HOLLY. Big gay following.

MEGAN. Massive.

HOLLY. Full of hunks.

BEN. Can't wait.

MEGAN. And you've got your flute.

HOLLY. I'm giving up the flute.

MEGAN. You've got rid of your flute, you've got your laptop and then you're just…

HOLLY. Singing? Maybe, I dunno.

MEGAN. Exactly.

Stood at the front and you're a bit scared to look up at first and then you do and Dean's just there, front row, in like, in his little hat, and you take a bit of heart from that. Cos even though you had a bit of a rocky start you've like explained how it was actually not your fault and he completely understands. Cos he's nice.

And then we just… I dunno we just.

HOLLY. What d'you reckon?

BEN. Worth a try?

MEGAN. Course it is. Of course.

HOLLY. Um, I've printed you the words so. Just do your best, sort of thing. It's nothing, it's shit but just, you know.

HOLLY gives MEGAN some words.

They sing.

It gets more sure of itself.

The garage fades away.

They are on an actual stage, doing an actual gig.

There are lots of fairy lights.

BEN.
Don't worry if you're fat.
Don't worry if you're gay.
Don't worry if you're too shy to sing,
If you want to wear a dress, that's okay
Wear anything.

EVERYONE.
We're not cool
We're not really cool but

We're in a band
An actual band.
We're not cool
We're not really cool but
We're in a band
An actual band.

HOLLY.

Don't worry if you're worried
Don't worry if you're sad
Don't worry if you don't fit in.
It's the ones who don't fit in who just
Fit in with each other.

EVERYONE.

We're not cool
We're not really cool but
We're in a band
An actual band.
We're not cool
We're not really cool but
We're in a band
An actual band.

BEN *and* HOLLY.

If you're angry we can listen, you can shout
Cos that is what your best mates do
Just shrug off all the worst of you
And sometimes dick about.
Dick about.

EVERYONE.

If you're not doing that well
If you're struggling a bit
If you've got nowhere to go
You can come and sit with us
We sing and dance and don't give a shit

We're not cool
We're not really cool but
We're in a band
An actual band.
We're not cool

We're not really cool but
We're in a band
An actual band.

Guitar stops. Big clap.

We're not cool
We're not really cool but
We're in a band
An actual band.

Massive ending.

We're not cool
We're not really cool but
We're in a band
An actual band.
We are in an actual band.

Other Titles in this Series

Mike Bartlett
BULL
GAME
AN INTERVENTION
KING CHARLES III
WILD

Jez Butterworth
JERUSALEM
JEZ BUTTERWORTH PLAYS: ONE
MOJO
THE NIGHT HERON
PARLOUR SONG
THE RIVER
THE WINTERLING

Melissa Bubnic
BEACHED
BOYS WILL BE BOYS

Caryl Churchill
BLUE HEART
CHURCHILL PLAYS: THREE
CHURCHILL PLAYS: FOUR
CHURCHILL: SHORTS
CLOUD NINE
DING DONG THE WICKED
A DREAM PLAY *after* Strindberg
DRUNK ENOUGH TO SAY
     I LOVE YOU?
ESCAPED ALONE
FAR AWAY
HERE WE GO
HOTEL
ICECREAM
LIGHT SHINING IN
     BUCKINGHAMSHIRE
LOVE AND INFORMATION
MAD FOREST
A NUMBER
PIGS AND DOGS
SEVEN JEWISH CHILDREN
THE SKRIKER
THIS IS A CHAIR
THYESTES *after* Seneca
TRAPS

Elinor Cook
THE GIRL'S GUIDE TO SAVING
     THE WORLD
IMAGE OF AN UNKNOWN YOUNG
     WOMAN
PILGRIMS

Samantha Ellis
CLING TO ME LIKE IVY
HOW TO DATE A FEMINIST

James Fritz
THE FALL
ROSS & RACHEL

Alan Harris
LOVE, LIES AND TAXIDERMY

Vicky Jones
THE ONE

Anna Jordan
CHICKEN SHOP
FREAK
YEN

Lucy Kirkwood
BEAUTY AND THE BEAST
     with Katie Mitchell
BLOODY WIMMIN
CHIMERICA
HEDDA *after* Ibsen
IT FELT EMPTY WHEN THE
     HEART WENT AT FIRST BUT
     IT IS ALRIGHT NOW
NSFW
TINDERBOX

Cordelia Lynn
LELA & CO.

Luke Norris
GOODBYE TO ALL THAT
GROWTH
SO HERE WE ARE

Stef Smith
HUMAN ANIMALS
REMOTE
SWALLOW

Sam Steiner
LEMONS LEMONS LEMONS
     LEMONS LEMONS

Jack Thorne
2ND MAY 1997
BUNNY
BURYING YOUR BROTHER IN
     THE PAVEMENT
HOPE
JACK THORNE PLAYS: ONE
LET THE RIGHT ONE IN
     after John Ajvide Lindqvist
MYDIDAE
THE SOLID LIFE OF SUGAR WATER
STACY & FANNY AND FAGGOT
WHEN YOU CURE ME

Phoebe Waller-Bridge
FLEABAG

Tom Wells
FOLK
JUMPERS FOR GOALPOSTS
THE KITCHEN SINK
ME, AS A PENGUIN

Camilla Whitehill
MR INCREDIBLE

A Nick Hern Book

Broken Biscuits first published as a paperback original in Great Britain in 2016 by Nick Hern Books Limited, The Glasshouse, 49a Goldhawk Road, London W12 8QP, in association with Paines Plough and Live Theatre, Newcastle

Broken Biscuits copyright © 2016 Tom Wells

Tom Wells has asserted his right to be identified as the author of this work

Cover image by Matt Humphrey

Designed and typeset by Nick Hern Books, London
Printed in the UK by CPI Books (UK) Ltd

A CIP catalogue record for this book is available from the British Library

ISBN 978 1 84842 596 5